THE PRIVATE MELVILLE

Also by Philip Young

Ernest Hemingway
Ernest Hemingway: A Reconsideration
The Hemingway Manuscripts: An Inventory, with Charles W. Mann
Three Bags Full: Essays in American Fiction
Revolutionary Ladies
Hawthorne's Secret: an Un-Told Tale

Philip Young

THE PRIVATE
MELVILLE

THE PENNSYLVANIA STATE UNIVERSITY PRESS
UNIVERSITY PARK, PENNSYLVANIA

Permission to reprint articles originally published in the following journals is gratefully acknowledged: Chapter 4, courtesy *College Literature*, © 1989 West Chester University; Chapter 7, courtesy *American Literature* and Duke University Press; and Chapter 9, courtesy *Studies in American Fiction*. Permission is also acknowledged for Chapter 8, which appears in *Studies in the American Renaissance 1990*, ed. Joel Myerson (Charlottesville: University of Virginia Press, 1990).

Library of Congress Cataloging-in-Publication Data

Young, Philip, 1918–1991
    The private Melville / Philip Young.
        p.   cm.
    Includes bibliographical references and index.
    ISBN 0-271-00857-1 (alk. paper)
    1. Melville, Herman, 1819–1891—Criticism and interpretation.
I. Title.
PS2387.Y68   1993
813'.3—dc20   92-15558
                                              CIP

Published by The Pennsylvania State University Press, Suite C, Barbara Building, University Park, PA 16802-1003

It is the policy of The Pennsylvania State University Press to use acid-free paper for the first printing of all clothbound books. Publications on uncoated stock satisfy the minimum requirements of American National Standard for Information Sciences—Permanence of Paper for Printed Library Materials, ANSI Z39.48–1984.

Philip Young
1918–1991

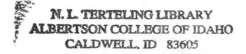

Contents

Editor's Note

Two days before he entered the hospital for cancer surgery from which he never recovered my husband completed the manuscript for *The Private Melville*. That immense gratification was his, as was the knowledge that the Penn State Press had, in a unanimous vote of its Editorial Committee, accepted the book for publication. As the Author's Widow I signed the contract and became style editor for the book which was as it should have been.

Over our nearly twenty-five years together I was Philip's first reader and his most demanding critic. I knew—really knew—his marvelously idiosyncratic voice, could pick it out in a crowd. And, of course, I'd had a part in *The Private Melville* from its inception.

The more I worked with the text, the more firmly persuaded I became that it was a work of genius. Philip's winsome way with cadence and comma had become second nature to me. What struck me with increasing force and awe was the depth of his disciplined and informed erudition, the soaring height, dissolving gentleness, and felicity of his prose. He had style, no doubt. I hope that I have been faithful to it.

Many have helped and encouraged me in what has been a true labor of love. Michael Begnal, Philip's colleague and friend, must be singled out, as must Richard Winslow III, "private investigator," collaborator, friend. Melville scholar Hershel Parker triggered my efforts with his initial and authoritative comments on the text. Philip Winsor, my "associate" at the Penn State Press, generously gave of his time, editorial experience, and sensitive understanding of the bittersweet task I was about. To them and all who have helped *The Private Melville* to live, my gratitude.

Katherine Young

State College, Pennsylvania
August 8, 1992

There is more power and beauty in the *well-kept secrets of one's self and one's thoughts,* than in the display of a whole heaven that one may have inside one . . .

—Maurice de Guérin
(underscored and
boxed by Melville)

Preface

In his later years Melville was living in New York City but a few doors from Edmund Clarence Stedman, a well-known writer. Yet even at home base Melville had "a hermit's reputation, and it was difficult to get more than a passing glimpse of his 'tall, stalwart figure' and grave preoccupied face." Even harder, as Hawthorne's son Julian discovered in 1883, was to get him to talk about the past. If letters from Hawthorne had existed, Melville said, "he had scrupulously destroyed them." As for memories of their times together, "he merely shook his head." The "chain of destructions," some of them witnessed bonfires, were chiefly of manuscripts and letters. Someone, probably he, burned every letter he wrote his mother; someone, probably they at his insistence, burned almost all he wrote brothers and sisters. His "youthful love-letters" went up in a fireplace. Letters to father, wife, and children are gone. *The Private Melville* is meant to suggest secrets. It was apparently after *Moby-Dick*, when he first thought of "posterity," that Melville "went private." He was never public again.

Privacy, as it appears to Melville here, is of three types. First are family matters the public had no business knowing about, such as the life story of a secret half-sister; next the story of the life of a cousin, Priscilla, model for the heroine of his novel *Pierre*, who scandalously "marries" her half-brother; then a history testing a rash claim made by Melville regarding the lineage of "hundreds" of ordinary New England families.

The second type concerns four Berkshire Tales that depend heavily on "private jokes" and thus have secret meaning that escaped the editors who printed them—as in many cases they have continued to evade critics and scholars who have imperfectly understood them (or in a couple of instances have not understood at all).

The third kind deals with two "fictions" so little understood that the meanings might as well be secret. A speech of Ahab's, first, that is called the "spiritual climax" of *Moby-Dick*. The other, Melville's very last fiction, a self-portrait in which he has gone pretty much unrecognized. But "Daniel Orme," dying, speaks for Melville on the decision to keep some matters private.

Backgrounds (Introduction)

I remember the instant's inception of this book. David R. Godine, Publisher, Boston, had advance copies of my *Hawthorne's Secret* (1984). Bill Goodman, my editor, as he had been years before in New York, had developed a warm literary friendship with Henry A. Murray, M.D., legendary figure whose nonprofessional passion since young manhood had been Melville. (He gave the founder of psychoanalysis a copy of *Moby-Dick* in 1925.) Interested in my new book, as Bill described it to him, Dr. Murray was given a copy. The response was extraordinary. He was very excited. Could he meet the author? I was already planning a trip to meet Godine, see Bill and the plant, eat seafood, walk yet again around the city. A meeting was arranged.

Thus Goodman and Young arrived for tea one afternoon at the Murrays' fine old-Harvard house, and were received by Nina Murray, unexpected bonus. Very soon, beaming and striding confidently behind his walker (he was ninety), appeared a handsome, erect man in a maroon ascot and well-cut (slightly soiled) linen jacket. He radiated enthusiasm, started at once talking about the *Hawthorne*, which he remembered in much detail. After that he caught his breath: what was I up to now?

I had just been talking to Bill about an 1832 letter, which led eventually to the first chapter of this book and more, that had not long been in print. It powerfully suggested that a woman called "A.M.A." with an older relative, "Mrs. B.," had called on the senior Melvills of Boston concerning money due one of them. A.M.A. was apparently the daughter of Allan Melvill, just deceased, Herman Melville's father. I was very excited about this. Long ago, on my first reading of Melville's *Pierre*, I had been gripped with the conviction that, like Pierre, Melville had an illegitimate sister. More, I had glimpsed (only) what might be the consequences of this knowledge for the brother and what he wrote. Beyond that, I had been hearing rumors to the effect that Dr. Murray knew the names of these women, even where they were buried. What I had been "up to" after the *Hawthorne* was finished was planned to be a book called *Dark Lady of the Republic* (in which Pierre's half-sister would figure). But now I had a great itch to know who these women were. Then I learned that this was Harry's great secret, very long held. What was I working on? I couldn't say I'd like to work on it, muttered something about being, uh, one of the many, including real Melvilleans, curious about those initials. I looked forward to the day when he would publish what he had learned.

I was uncomfortable. But the turn of topic delighted Harry. His face, already animated, lit up. Still standing, he took another stride. "Aha!" he said as if he had hit a jackpot. Then, relishing the syllables, "Ann Middleton Allen and Martha Bent!" (A short cut.) He talked more about the women, supplying facts of considerable interest, and answered questions freely. He asked if I had been analyzed (no). Time passed swiftly, then Mrs. Murray somehow signed that we should not tire him further. Yes, I promised, I would return as soon as I got back to Cambridge, as I did, and Bill would return sooner. The Goodmans and I went off to dinner, and I flew home in the morning. Not before a quick stop at the Boston Public Library, whose catalogue listed genealogies of both American Bents and Allens.

These are not generally available in university libraries, and were photocopied for me by Richard E. Winslow III, to whom I am indebted for more voluntary research and related effort than I can now remember. He helped mightily with *Hawthorne's Secret*, which is inscribed to him, and shared in the excitement of a major discovery we jointly made concerning the writer's Salem ancestors. (I did tell Dick about my new knowledge, which was about as risky as confiding it to a clam.)

I got back to 22 Frances Avenue all right, and told Dr. Murray of a minor discovery linking Melville's father and Ann Bent (the actual "Mrs. B.") that I'd made in the Houghton Library. He became agitated, anxious: was I going to publish it? Of course not, it was for him, if he wanted it. (He used and acknowledged it but was not easy. He didn't know how gladly I wolde lerne and pass it along.)

Early 1985 brought developments. Harry wrote of his most recent stroke; not all his neurons were in tune, he said. Next time I saw him he was bedridden but clearheaded as ever, for all I could see. I also thought he was holding something back. He liked to surprise people, as he had astonished me. And surely he knew that if he were to see his discoveries in print it was time. Suddenly, in February, there it was: a piece called "Allan Melvill's By-Blow" in *Melville Society EXTRACTS*. Only six pages, it is a packed, lucid summary of research begun in the mid-1940s when Charles Olson, working on *Call Me Ishmael*, found the letter of 1832, the source of the whole business, in the archives of Chief Justice Lemuel Shaw, eventually Herman's father-in-law. (Seeing no use for it in his book Olson passed a copy along to Murray; it was rediscovered and printed in 1977, but the identity of the women remained secret.)

I heard more from Harry; he wrote (undated) of yet a third stroke, which had him "out of commission for a while. Only my hand-writing has been unimpaired," as it appeared. Then there was a letter of April 5, 1985. It had the usual complimentary close, "Salvos to you! / Harry." But it had ended "Write me! I'm nearly through." I had and did, especially about his essay, "the best thing of its kind I ever read."

I don't think he got back into working condition, but I didn't hear anything. Then in the *New York Times*, June 24, 1988, I saw that he had died at ninety-five of pneumonia. He had been, the paper said, "among other things, one of the early American-born psychoanalysts [I hadn't known that], a selector of agents for the Office of Strategic Services in World War II, a scholar and leading authority on the life and works of Herman Melville." A great many disparate "other things" were mentioned.

Once "By-Blow" had appeared and one acknowledged an enormous debt to it, he felt free to see what he could discover for himself. I did, and so did Winslow, passing things along to me. First I wrote "Small World: Emerson, Longfellow, and Melville's Secret Sister," which appeared in the *New England Quarterly* in September 1987. It was an interesting story and well received—until August 1989, when

I learned that *my* Ann Tracy (A.M.A. had married Nathaniel Tracy, of a distinguished Newburyport family) was not *the* Ann Tracy of Newburyport who, as I had reported, had entertaining exchanges with R. W. Emerson's Aunt Mary, and with Emerson himself.[1] I have notified *NEQ* of the considerable mistake, apologized for it, and on behalf of Winslow, and for *The Private Melville* have rewritten the chapter, removing erroneous material and now calling it "History of a Secret Sister." The Longfellow connection remains.

II

While I was researching and writing these chapters, it was slow to dawn on me that if they became a Melville book it would probably be the first to investigate the importance of a hidden sibling to a half-brother's life and work. In any event, if *Pierre* is any guide—at special times it does ring true—the news, when it hit Herman, was terrible. Like Pierre, he had as a boy idolized his pious father; like Pierre, he somewhat confused him with deity. For Pierre, destruction of belief in the one collapsed faith in both. As I worked along, this lasting trauma kept surfacing.

Three chapters dealing with Family Matters open this book, and look into ways the fact of this little known woman branch out. First an attempt on her life story relates in more detail than Dr. Murray included a biography of the actual half-sister, Ann Middleton Allen (1798–1869), who fared better than might be expected of a girl of the time and place born out of wedlock to parents who went their separate ways before she was born. Then an essay on *Pierre* centers

1. The mistake was pointed out to me in 1989 by Nancy Craig Simmons of Virginia Polytechnic Institute and State University. Ann M. Tracy, Mrs. Nathaniel Tracy, was apparently in Newburyport at the time, in 1843, because of the fatal illness of her husband's son, whose home was there. So, however, was Ann B. Tracy, wife of the Rev. Thomas Tracy. (Winslow and I were aware of him but unaware of a wife; Winslow did a great deal of careful research in Newburyport; I searched Directories of the place without ever encountering her.) Ms. Simmons apparently did not have her Ann's signature, but I did, from a letter she wrote Emerson. Winslow had furnished a photocopy of a signed codicil Ann M. Tracy had appended to her will. The signatures proved Professor Simmons right.

on the "real life" person I identify as the original for the portrait of the unreal Isabel, heroine of the novel.

The third piece in this section is a spin-off, testing a rash claim made by an enthusiastic author at the start of *Pierre* regarding the traceable lineage of "hundreds" of ordinary New England families. It is a history of Ann M. Allen's ancestors. Not her father's, the genealogy of American Melvilles being well established. Rather of the often obscure forebears of her mother, whose father was a New England Bent, the mother a New England Middleton.

III

While this work was in progress, or stuck at one point or another, I undertook a massive program of rereading Melville. Not everything, as it turned out, but a great deal. I also read or reread a good deal that has been written about him and his work. The purpose was to discover where significant things remained to be said. Considering the amazing amount of work—some of it really valuable—that has been done on Melville, it is remarkable that obvious holes are to be found. (Who would believe that a famous speech by Ahab has never been explained? Or that there is nothing approaching an intelligent reading of Melville's moving last tale, "Daniel Orme"?)

Indeed I found that four closely related and quite well-known stories ("Tales of the Berkshire Bishopric") all contain crucial symbolism that has never been made wholly clear—or, in one case, even detected. "Family Matters" would in Melville's mind be classified Secret. The Berkshire Tales were available to anyone who could get hold of them, but were Confidential. This because the author entrusted their meaning to the discreet few who could both enjoy and comprehend the larger significance of "private jokes."

"The Berkshire Bishopric" is a very small private joke based on an authorial secret that has remained secret: the true identity of the terroristic "Lightning-Rod Man," a caricature of a prominent clergyman of Melville's day known as "a sort of Bishop" of the diocese around Pittsfield, where Melville lived and wrote just outside town at

Arrowhead. The minister was also author of an excessively long-lived bestseller called *The Student's Manual*, whose male readers were drawn in horror to a small section that focused on a phallic phobia. The title of this distinct group of stories hopes to suggest the sexual electricity that, in the four tales, charged the region they are set in.

The most private of them, "Tartarus" for short, is the richest, most powerful, many-sided, and deepest. It is a secret masterpiece. Sexual symbolism of great originality, fully absorbed myth and allegory, the resonant presence of Dante, a riveting sleigh ride— everything leads to a stated but misunderstood "point." One secret, hidden out of sight, is yet again fatherhood. But this time the father is Herman Melville.

IV

"Fathers and Sons" forces together two unlike forms of "fiction." First is a blasphemous, occasionally enigmatic speech delivered by Ahab over a wrecked deck under corposant light. Among the mighty gods he summons, defies, and worships appears again the irrepressible Allan Melvill, who for once is defied worshipfully. It is the end of something, a final agony Ahab didn't survive.

"Daniel Orme" is the nearly unknown coda to all of Melville, where in the guise of an exhausted ex-seaman the writer puts his solitary bones to rest. Ahab, in his speech, took the Almighty Father down a peg, but was willing to kneel before the god of love. Daniel Orme has an indelible tattoo of the crucifixion on his breast, but it is slashed by a whitish scar that will not fade either. Something has cancelled the sign of the Son on the cross. There is nothing left to destroy. But then Melville brings the matter of personal secrecy to a conclusion, along with Orme's (and his own) long life. Mention is made of a Calvinist chaplain who inferred "some dark deed" in the sailor's past. And just as the tale closes, Melville admits that Orme's silence and freakish nervous behavior may trace to "something dark that he chose to keep to himself." It is clear that in death Orme/Melville had a secret he's still not telling. There is "power and beauty" in that.

FAMILY MATTERS

1

History of a Secret Sister

Where is the foundling's father hidden? Our souls are like
those orphans whose unwedded mothers die in bearing
them; the secret of their paternity lies in their grave, and we
must there to learn it.

—Moby-Dick

I

In a 1903 biography of his father, Julian Hawthorne—discounting
Herman Melville's claim that "there was a secret in [Nathaniel's] life
which had never been revealed, and which accounted for the gloomy
passages in his books"—remarked coolly that "there were many
secrets untold in [Melville's] own career."[1] Not that Hawthorne's son
knew much about Melville secrets. But surely the collapsed life of
this famous sailor-whaler-writer, now old, pale, terribly nervous,
nearly silent, and all but forgotten on a quiet street in a great city,
hid some.

Over a century has passed since Julian's 1883 interview with
Melville. For more than half that time, marvelous energies have been
expended on his life and work. Secrets remain. A very important
one, however, has been freshly uncovered. At ninety-two the astonishing Henry A. Murray, M.D.—biochemist turned psychoanalyti-
cally bent Harvard psychologist and, among other callings, longtime
leading Melvillean—has published information he had sat on for
decades. Curious news it was, too, having been vigorously denied
long in advance of its disclosure.

1. Julian Hawthorne, *Hawthorne and His Circle* (New York: Harper & Brothers, 1903), 33.
On Hawthorne, see my *Hawthorne's Secret: An Untold Tale* (Boston: David R. Godine, 1984).

In 1852, as Melville was writing his novel *Pierre*, family and friends, aware that "a sick man [was] writing of some matters known to be true," feared that more might be assumed true than was.[2] Was he suggesting that his own father, Allan, like Pierre's in the book, had in his youth sired an illegitimate daughter? Perish the thought.

Robert Forsythe set out to do just that: "There is no evidence whatsoever for connecting the story of Isabel's mother"—Isabel is Pierre's half-sister—"with any happening in the life of Allan Melville."[3] Yet in 1951 William H. Gilman could remark that "It has been popular to hint that Allan's youthful wanderings yielded many a pleasant and secret amour and even a natural daughter."[4] In support he cites early books on the famous son by Lewis Mumford, Raymond Weaver, and the Frenchman Jean Simon. Here the story becomes more curious.

Mumford contradicts Gilman flat out: if Allan's bachelor adventures left any "tell tale traces," we have no better reason for thinking so than that there is a crack in the image of Pierre's father.[5] Weaver is more opaque: Allan "may have been annointed in mortality" (whatever that means), but "all surviving evidence" presents him as "a model of rigid decorum."[6] Jean Simon has much more to say.[7] He speculates on Allan's trips to France (where Isabel was born of a French mother). He effectively dismisses a letter Allan wrote his wife from Paris in which he boasts of his perfect fidelity. More surprising, Simon passes on a longtime suspicion of Murray's: that while living as a young man in Paris with his brother Thomas and his exotic wife Françoise, Allan fathered one of her several children. (Very likely Murray had in mind Priscilla, Melville's French-born older cousin, whom he came to know and whom Isabel resembles. In the

2. Eleanor Melville Metcalf, *Herman Melville: Cycle and Epicycle* (Cambridge: Harvard University Press, 1953), 135.

3. *Pierre; or, The Ambiguities*, ed. Robert S. Forsythe (New York: Alfred A. Knopf, 1930), xxii.

4. William H. Gilman, *Melville's Early Life and "Redburn"* (New York: New York University Press, 1951), 8.

5. Lewis Mumford, *Herman Melville* (New York: Harcourt, Brace & Co., 1929), 14.

6. Raymond Weaver, *Herman Melville, Mariner and Mystic* (New York: George H. Doran & Co., 1921), 56–57.

7. Jean Simon, *Herman Melville: Marin, metaphysicien et poete* (Paris: Boivin & Cie, 1939), 28–29.

end, Simon reports, Murray renounced the hypothesis.) Finally Simon repeats what he calls a circulating rumor (*bruit*), told him by Raymond Weaver, who judged it *très vraisemblable*: that after Allan's death a woman and her daughter presented themselves to "the family," exacted *une somme assez ronde*, and then departed.

This *bruit* had carried over a hundred years when Simon picked it up. But what Gilman really missed in all this was, again, Murray, who did more than "hint" that Pierre's fatal discovery was no invention. In 1949, in an extraordinary introduction to *Pierre*, he wrote plainly of the hero's discovery that he has a secret sister: "That Melville was confronted by an equivalent situation in his own life is a conclusion that seems warranted by the evidence, but this is not the place to marshal it."[8]

The evidence—what Murray calls "the Telltale Letter" of 1832 from Thomas Melville, Jr., Allan's brother, then back in America, to Chief Justice Lemuel Shaw, a close family friend—is persuasive.[9] This document powerfully suggests that Weaver's ancient gossip was pretty close to the mark—that one "Mrs. A.M.A." of Boston was Allan Melvill's "by-blow" and that "Mrs. B." was her mother (a natural though mistaken inference). The women had called at the house of Allan's father, Major Thomas Melvill, who was not at home, in a doomed search for money apparently promised the fatherless daughter, now a grown woman, and never paid. (And Allan dead, totally bankrupt.) Thomas, who did not doubt the justice of the claim, gave Mrs. B. "some money" (he had very little). From what he saw of A.M.A., he wrote, "I thought her quite an interesting young person,—that it was most unfortunate she had not been brought up different."

For nearly forty years, Murray writes, he set the letter aside "for seasoning." This obscure treatment aborted in 1977 when a younger scholar, Amy Puett Emmers, who rediscovered the letter in Lemuel Shaw's archives, understood and published it.[10] Yet nothing save

8. *Pierre; or, The Ambiguities*, ed. Henry A. Murray (New York: Hendrick's House, 1949), xlvi.

9. Henry A. Murray et al., "Allan Melvill's By-Blow," *Melville Society Extracts* 61 (February 1985): 1–6.

10. Amy Puett Emmers, "Melville's Closet Skeleton: A New Letter About the Illegitimacy Incident in *Pierre*," in *Studies in the American Renaissance, 1977* (Boston: Twayne, 1978), 339–42. Dr. Murray also prints the letter.

initials identified the women. Murray, a shrewd detective with a Boston Directory for 1833, had long since found them out. Neither woman was married, the titles being a courtesy of the time and Melvill's. The daughter was Ann Middleton Allen, and "B" was her foster mother and aunt, Ann Bent, a successful businesswoman of the town.[11]

Enter the genealogies, which Murray also consulted. Ann Bent had herself arrived a little "soon." The real mother of Herman Melville's half-sister was Martha Bent of Canton, Massachusetts, fourth daughter of Rufus Bent and the widowed Ann Middleton, daughter of a reputable Scotsman of Boston.[12] At the time of her misadventure in 1797, Martha was probably helping out at her sister's shop, which specialized in French goods. The store was at 56 Marlboro Street, later redesignated 214 Washington. Quarters for the women were above it. Done with his schooling, Allan was very likely living with his parents at 20 Green Street, no great distance away.

Born in Boston on April 7, 1782, Allan had been brought up to be pious, patriotic, and upright. At school he was interested in literature and style. Not much is known of his adolescent years. It is generally unknown that as early as December 1805 he was elaborately advertising "French Goods For Sale by ALLAN MELVILL at No. 2, Suffolk Buildings, Congress-street" in the *Boston Gazette*. Congress Street ran roughly parallel to Marlboro, and only a couple of blocks over. Allan remained in that business until he moved to New York in 1814.

As a competitor of Ann Bent's, Allan surely laid eyes on his daughter, or she on him, after she became apprenticed to her aunt in 1808. Murray suspects Allan may have been employed at Bent's himself when he impregnated Martha, who was then twenty-one. If it is assumed that her child was carried to term, conception would have occurred on or about July 11, 1797—at which time the father was fifteen years and three months old. On December 12, 1797,

11. It may seem odd that Ann Bent and Ann Middleton Allen should have called on the Melvills in search of money they do not appear to have needed. It was probably a matter of principle with them—a last attempt to see justice done, a very old debt paid—an act of female courage.

12. Allen H. Bent, *The Bent Family in America* (Boston: David Clapp & Son, 1900), 46.

Martha, now back in Canton, a few miles south of Boston, married Bethuel Allen of nearby Stoughton, as the Canton town records show (Murray's "By-Blow," 3). But for all his searching, Murray never did discover any sort of notice of the birth of the child. Canton records ignore it; none of the many Allen children are mentioned in Bent's exhaustive genealogy of the family.

If, however, A.B.A.'s death certificate is accurate in saying she was seventy-one years, five months, nineteen days old when she died (September 30, 1869), she was born on April 11, 1798. But this date went unverified until September 1990 when Richard E. Winslow III of Rye, New Hampshire, after years of helping research matters here at hand, visited the New England Historic Genealogical Society in Boston, just across the Charles from Harry's house in Cambridge, and found the title page of Bethuel's family Bible. Across the top of the sheet Bethuel's hand wrote bold and clear: "Ann M. Allen Born April 11, 1798." Other entries beneath fill the sheet. Thus there is documentary evidence that the woman was born, and when. More significant, Martha Bent's new husband acted with dignity and taste.

An obsessive traveler, Allan at nineteen was sent on the grand tour, during which he spent twenty months in Paris with his prospering brother Thomas. After marrying in 1814 and opening his business on Pearl Street in New York, where Herman was born, he continued to move about. Every summer he took his growing family out of the pestilential heat. By the time he was three, Herman and the others went by packet and private carriage to visit his grandparents in Boston. In other summers they did likewise. Thus Allan was repeatedly in Boston when his daughter, by then in her twenties, was as well. Moreover, a letter recently discovered by the present writer in the Melville Papers at Harvard, dated December 23, 1823, shows that Allan, through his father, was still in touch with Ann Bent regarding a business debt of $77.74.[13]

Much remains to be discovered of A.M.A.'s story and of her family background, searched later in this book. The literary significance of Melville's knowledge of her existence turns out to be great. There is

13. In "By-Blow" the figure was mistranscribed as $7,774, and misinterpreted as being owed *by* Allan Melvill, not *to* him.

no documentary evidence to show when Herman learned he had a half-sister, but the early chapters of *Pierre* are remarkably autobiographical. Pierre is told of his Isabel by his Aunt Dorothea in their family mansion in the Berkshires. It is easily recognized today as the estate at Pittsfield purchased in 1816 by Major Melvill, his grandfather, and then occupied by the family of the major's son Thomas, Herman's uncle, and Mary, his second wife. Herman lived and worked there in the summer of 1837, when Thomas himself had left for Galena, Illinois, anticipating the removal of his family there. Herman was fond of his father's brother, and came to admire the new Mrs. Melvill. It is quite possible that sometime during this period he learned of Thomas's 1832 trip to Boston and the meeting with A.B. and A.M.A. from his Aunt Mary. But the object here is to establish a larger place for Melville's hidden sister in the small world of Boston, and to develop some sense of her as a human being.

II

By 1834 Ralph Waldo Emerson had lost his first wife, resigned his pastorate, and returned from a trip to Europe but had not really begun his career as a writer. In Boston he took a room at 276 Washington Street not far from A.M.A. and A.B. at 214. But in April he wrote his brother William that he and his mother would "probably live at Newton at Mrs. Allens. I carry . . . a head preposterously stuffed with projects of thoughts studies books philanthropies."[14] The Allens rented rooms.

Murray has already pointed out that this is the Mrs. Allen who gave birth to Allan Melvill's first child thirty-six years earlier. Her husband Bethuel was a descendant of Lewis Allen, an early settler of what is now Weston, west of Cambridge. Martha's first children were apparently born in Canton, though not recorded there. A receipt signed by Paul in the Revere Family Papers for money paid

14. *The Letters of Ralph Waldo Emerson*, ed. Ralph L. Rusk, 6 vols. (New York: Columbia University Press, 1939), 1:409.

Bethuel indicates that he was still in Canton in 1803. But in 1805 Mr. Allen purchased a pew in the First Congregational Church of West Newton, a few miles northwest of Canton, although it was not until 1822 that he and his wife were baptized into it. (The children's names are recorded except for Ann Allen's—not, it would appear, because of her origin, as Murray suggests, but because she had gone to live and work with her Aunt Bent in Boston fourteen years previously.) Bethuel had somehow acquired (from his father?) "a large farm" in Newton with a "quiet old farmhouse" at what is now 227 Woodward Street. It was a good-looking and substantial saltbox, as an old printed sketch attests.[15]

"Why have you not been out here to see the pines & the hermit?" wrote Emerson, then living at the farm with his mother in the summer of 1834:

> It is calm as eternity out here, & will give you lively ideas of the same. These sleepy hollows full of savins & cinquefoils seem to utter a quiet satire at the ways & politics of men. I think the robin and finch the only philosophers. . . . 'Tis deep Sunday in this woodcocks nest of ours from one end of the week to the other—times & seasons get lost here sun & stars make all the difference of night & day.[16]

In Murray's essay he dismisses the Newton interlude as "a pleasant summer." It was, more to the point, a fruitful season. Emerson was warming up for his first book, *Nature* (1836), and several thoughts that would appear in it were earlier expressed at Newton. He was pointing toward the most famous of his early essays, "The American Scholar" and "Self-Reliance" ("21 May. I will trust my instincts"). He recorded nothing of Martha Allen or of practically anyone else, save writers, but he did note: "April 26, Newton. The muses love the woods & I have come hither to court the awful Powers in this sober solitude."[17] Here too he wrote the first of his best-known poems,

---

15. The print appears in M. F. Sweetser's *King's Handbook of Newton, Massachusetts* (Boston: Moses King Corp., 1889). See Murray's "By-Blow," 4.

16. Emerson, *Letters*, 1:415.

17. *The Journals and Miscellaneous Notebooks* of Ralph Waldo Emerson, vol. 4, ed. Alfred R. Ferguson (Cambridge: Harvard University Press, 1964), 292, 280.

"The Rhodora," six lines of which—ending, "if eyes were made for seeing, / Then Beauty is its own excuse for being"—are still in *Bartlett's Familiar Quotations*.

Emerson, a biographer observes, was "searching tirelessly for genius." But the Shock of Recognition never traveled from Boston to New York—or from Concord to Pittsfield. Radically though not entirely different, Melville could write of Emerson, "Say what you will, he's a great man." Melville went to hear a lecture in Boston; he read two volumes of essays, more prose, and some poetry. Emerson owned a copy of *Typee* and wrote his name in it. No one knows if he ever heard of *Moby-Dick*. (He disparaged novels.)

It is completely unlikely, further, that Emerson could have known that he had roomed and boarded with the mother of the novelist's sister. Nor is it likely that if he ever crossed paths with the sister herself he would have discovered her relationship to his former landlady. At the start of 1843, A.M.A. was forty-five, single, and employed in the business at Boston from which Ann Bent had recently retired. On October 14, 1844, Herman Melville was discharged from the navy at Boston after a most protracted "whaling voyage." Perhaps he wondered about the woman of that town he had heard about—who might still be in the store, perhaps doomed to it—whatever. He had really nothing of any importance to do; conceivably he walked over to Washington Street and looked around. But by then Ann Middleton Allen had married a widower named Tracy, and had moved to a new address.

III

More might be known of Ann Middleton Allen's life before she married than has in fact been learned. Since childhood her existence must have related to Ann Bent. A remarkable woman, Ann Bent was born in poverty, but let out to work in two advantaged homes; she early became a schoolteacher in nearby Milton. Then, still young, she opened a successful and long-lived ladies' imported-goods shop on Marlboro Street, where a part of Filene's is still in business. It is simplest to infer that she inherited her talents and energy from her mother, Ann Middleton, of a prominent Scottish family, for whom her niece was named.

In the summer of 1826 the Bent-Allen household grew by one when Mary Lovell Pickard, daughter of an English merchant of Boston who had helped stock Ann's start in business, returned from a visit to England. Mary and A.M.A. were the same age, and through common descent from Middletons the women were closely related. Mary Pickard's mother, a Middleton, had married James Lovell, famous Patriot orator, mathematician, linguist, and captured Rebel spy who became a contentious, durable Congressman. (He was the son of the equally famous "Master Lovell" of Boston Latin, a firm Loyalist.) So obscure that there is apparently no formal record of her birth, Melville's half-sister was well connected.

These women were in turn connected with the liveliest institution of their time and place. Newly back from England, Mary Pickard had already been swayed by the powerful sermon of a Unitarian pastor, the Reverend Henry Ware, Jr., widowed, of the Second or Old North Church ("One if by land, and two if by sea" related to another Old North Church). Mary was oppressed by "solemn," "awful" thoughts of putting "lone Polly Pickard" behind her. Within six months, writes her eventual biographer, "The marriage of the REV. HENRY WARE, Jr., and MARY L. PICKARD took place at the house of Miss Bent in Boston, on the 11th of June, 1827, Dr. Gannett uniting and blessing them." (Ezra Stiles Gannett, younger than William Ellery Channing or Ware, would become Boston's Unitarian leader.) After a short trip the Wares moved into a house near his church, and "Miss ——— was there to receive her."

The biographer here was Edward B. Hall, whose *Memoir of Mary L. Ware* (1853) would make her better known than her husband. He was never healthy; she long cared for him—and for an astonishing number of sick and dying relatives, among others. The Wares traveled for his health, and Mary never forgot Miss ———; she wrote "Dear Ann" letters from London asking for news of Channing's latest sermons. In Rome she had a daughter, Ann Bent Ware. She ended her days in Milton, very near where Ann Bent's father was born. She gets full treatment—along with Margaret Fuller, Harriet

Beecher Stowe, and Louisa May Alcott—as a "Protestant saint" in Seth Curtis Beach's *Daughters of the Puritans* (1905). Emerson had a copy of the *Memoir* in his library, but none of Ware's many books.

Emerson had of course been close to the Unitarian scene. Gannett was a year ahead of him at Harvard. When needed, Emerson filled in by preaching for Ware, and when the pastor's health failed to improve in 1830, Emerson became the new minister. Next year Ellen Emerson, his first wife, died at nineteen; Ware preached the funeral sermon. Back in 1822 Ware had probably been the first person to publish Emerson.

But "our Bishop," as Emerson dubbed him, was William Ellery Channing. He was a powerful figure; "women in particular" were drawn to him, and there is a notable list of such: Dorothea Dix, social and penal reformer; Harriet Martineau, enormously popular English writer in Boston; Lydia Child, novelist and crusader; Catherine Sedwick, compared to Scott and Cooper; Elizabeth Peabody, pioneer educator and once Channing's "almost idolatrous" secretary. (Hawthorne, her brother-in-law, remarked that Channing was one of those "clever young men whom Mr. Emerson . . . is continually picking up by way of a genius.")

No doubt that a hunger for intellectual stimulation was abroad, and many were drawn to Channing's doctrine of self-culture. Ann Bent was devoted to him, and her *Boston Evening Transcript* obituary called her one of Channing's "most valued parishioners." Elizabeth Anthony Dexter in *Career Women of America, 1776–1840* (1950) sees her as "the center of a wide circle of friends, among whom were many of the leading literati and reformers of the day." When Mary Pickard arrived at her household as a communicant of Trinity Church and daughter of an English Episcopalian, she was "led by the hand" of Ann Bent, Hall writes, "as if by the hand of a mother," directly to Channing.

Boston was in "the gestation period" of American feminism. The Bent circle doubtless overlapped the better-known "Channing Circle," whose members were all Unitarian women, their "guiding light" Ezra Stiles Gannett, who was more of a ruler. The Bent group most likely had built-in leadership. The question is where Ann Middleton Allen was to be found in the broad picture.

There is not a clue save in action, which was unambiguous. Unitarianism had peaked by 1842, when Channing died. In 1843, after thirty-five years in her foster-mother's quarters and shop, A.M.A. up and married a conservative Episcopalian stockbroker from Newburyport, Treasurer of the Boston Merchant's Exchange and a founder of the Boston Stock Exchange. She was not joined to Nathaniel Tracy by Unitarian leadership, or at Trinity Church; the marriage was recorded at Boston City Hall on April 23 (Murray, 6). The Tracys moved into a stunning and fashionable residence, designed by Bulfinch, in the Tontine Crescent at 11 Franklin Place. It was an eye-filling turnabout. It also offered a privileged visit to past glories and a new life.

A telling fact is that Ann's husband was the son of *the* Nathaniel Tracy, Harvard '69, who had built one of the great American fortunes in privateering before losing it and his enormous fleet in the Revolutionary War, which he substantially helped finance out of his partisan pocket. In prosperity he was no more famed for his ships than his houses, starting with the mansion his father built for him when he married—now the Newburyport Public Library—where, among many of the great, he entertained George Washington. He owned as well the esteemed Vassall (later Craigie) House in Cambridge. It was said he could travel from Newburyport to Virginia and sleep every night under his own roof.[18]

Major Thomas Melvill, Herman's grandfather, was Princeton '69, but when awarded an honorary degree from Harvard, he was placed in Tracy's small class. Thus Ann Tracy's deceased father-in-law and her biological grandfather had been classmates of a sort. For that matter, Major Melvill and her husband Nathaniel must have known each other, both having been officials (as was Nathaniel Hawthorne) of the Boston Custom House in the 1830s. Earlier both Ann's husband Tracy and her grandfather Melvill had figured together in Boston town meetings. In the 1822 balloting for the new city government at Faneuil Hall, each received two endorsements in the heavy voting for councillors and senators for the District of Suffolk.

18. See Thomas Amory Lee, "The Tracy Family of Newburyport," *Essex Institute Historical Collections* 57 (January 1921): 57–74.

(Lemuel Shaw, eventually Herman Melville's father-in-law, got 2,305 votes.) Also crossing paths at Fanueil Hall were both of Ann Tracy's grandfathers, paternal and maternal. In 1784, immediately after Major Melvill was excused as fire warden, Martha Bent's father Rufus was voted and sworn a constable. And there was contact in the succeeding generation. Ann Tracy's future husband Nathaniel was clearly known to her father Allan, who in 1829 wrote *his* father Thomas about some money due him. "Not being rec I have written to him this day . . . to the care of N Tracy, requesting him to enclose me a check."[19]

On his sixty-ninth birthday Emerson stood on Summer Street in Boston, at the old parsonage where he was born, near the pasture where he drove the cows mornings—and near the shop Miss Bent had opened before he existed. He was thinking of people of Boston's past as he had learned of them from his Aunt Mary. "It is now a hundred years since she was born," he wrote in his *Journals* (16:274), "and the founders of the oldest families that are still notable were known to her as retail-merchants, milleners, tailors," as well as professionals. The thought was no farther from the Bent-Allens than he from their store, now operated by William Henry Allen, Bethuel and Martha's youngest, a prominent businessman. He lived in Canton, where Ann Bent had died at eighty-eight in the home of a sister.

Most of what Emerson could see on that May morning of 1872 was gone in six months, obliterated by the Great Fire of Boston, November 9–10. Summer Street is where it started. It took enough of Washington Street to consume the Bent store and dwellings, and the *Transcript* building, before being "driven off." Franklin Place, only a block from Summer, was in the heart of it. Even the great stone walls were destroyed—not those of the Bulfinch buildings, already torn down for expanding commerce, but their successors. All of Trinity Church was gone but the tower, and everything from Washington Street all the way to the wharves and the water's edge.

19. Allan Melvill to Thomas Melvill, Sr., September 12, 1829, Melville Papers, Houghton Library, Harvard University.

IV

In a manner of speaking, Emerson's body outlived his mind. In 1882 his daughter Ellen took him to Longfellow's funeral at his home in Cambridge, where her father had occasionally dined. After twice visiting the open coffin he asked, "Where are we? What house? And who is the sleeper?"[20] What house indeed? As a widower and Harvard professor, Longfellow had taken two large rooms in it forty-five years earlier—then a third and a kitchen. He felt like an Italian prince in a villa. Six years later he married Fanny Appleton, the beautiful second Mrs. Longfellow, just after Ann Allen became the second Mrs. Tracy. The wedding was held at the Appleton house on Beacon Street; Ezra Stiles Gannett presided, as he had at Ann Bent's for the Wares. By the light of a full moon, wrote the bride, the newlyweds approached "Castle Craigie" on Brattle Street, where the groom had been living. The widow Craigie had died; Nathan Appleton, Fanny's father, had promised the couple a house. Not this one. He would have preferred something newer. But for $10,000 he bought an estate. There Longfellow became the best-known American poet and Fanny bore six children. Then she died when her dress caught fire and her husband could not smother the flames. The funeral procession made its way to Mount Auburn Cemetery, as Allens and Tracys were doing. Dr. Gannett read a different service, and Nathan died next day.

While Fanny lived, Longfellow counted his residence a paradise. How "noble an inheritance," she wrote, where "Washington dwelt in every room." So, of course, had others. The poet addressed an unidentified acquaintance in June 1845:

> MY DEAR SIR,
> Perhaps you remember some conversation we had together a year or so ago about an ancestor of yours who once occupied Cragie [sic] House. I am now making a little record

20. Ralph L. Rusk, *The Life of Ralph Waldo Emerson* (New York: Charles Scribner's Sons, 1949), 506.

of the persons who have lived here: and should be obliged to you if you would send me some account of him; when and how long he lived here &c.—anything that might be interesting.

> Yours very Truly,
> Henry W. Longfellow[21]

Then in faint pencil it reads: "Show this to the Tracys and ask them about their father."

Clearly Longfellow was in easy touch with Ann and Nathaniel Tracy and knew that the latter's father had owned the mansion and grounds, as he did from 1781 to 1786. Originally the Vassall House, it was built about 1759—an "elegant and spacious mansion" on about one hundred fifty acres outside Cambridge. The Vassalls were an old family, having come to the province in 1635. But they remained "loyal," and when loyalist property was confiscated, a battalion from Marblehead was billeted in the house and grounds. George Washington, his wife and staff had lived there through the eight-month siege of Boston. After him came a merchant named Russell and then Dr. Andrew Craigie, who (according to Samuel Adams Drake) "amassed a very large fortune as apothecary general to the Continental army." Craigie entertained as royally as Tracy. After his death his widow rented apartments to gentlemen. Craigie-Longfellow House is now a National Historic Site.

If they never learned of it, as is almost surely the case, the Longfellows would have been really interested to know of Ann Tracy's relationship to Herman Melville. When *Typee* was new, Fanny read it aloud to her husband, who was having trouble with his eyes. He liked it very well. Next summer they tackled *Omoo*. She was a Bostonian. "I understand," she wrote her father, "The author is engaged to a daughter of Judge Shaw. After his flirtations with South Sea beauties it is a peculiar choice (in her)."[22] At that time the Longfellows rented for the summer another great house, which became known as

21. *The Letters of Henry Wadsworth Longfellow*, ed. Andrew Hilen, vol. 3, 1844–56 (Cambridge: Belknap Press of Harvard University Press, 1972), 77–78.

22. *Mrs. Longfellow: Selected Letters and Journals of Fanny Appleton Longfellow*, ed. Edward Wagenknecht (New York: Longmans, Green, 1956), 132.

Broadhall, in Pittsfield. Purchased in 1816 by Major Thomas Melvill, it is now the Pittsfield Country Club. This is where Herman had lived and farmed. Married, he and Shaw's daughter Elizabeth would summer here as well. "A stately old house," Longfellow observed, "with rooms large as our own at home." They called it Melville Hall, Typee Valley. On a November evening in 1851 the poet would read in a new "very wild, strange and interesting book," *Moby-Dick*.

He would have been little less interested in Ann Tracy's family background for another reason. It had to do with the old Red Horse Inn, some twenty miles west of Cambridge, near Sudbury. In the fall of 1862 he drove out to see the place, "a rambling tumble-down old building, two hundred years old; and till now in the family of Howes, who have kept an inn for 175 years . . . a port of call for all travellers from Boston westward."[23]

The poet was after local color, although he'd already written the Prelude to *Tales of a Wayside Inn*, in which he described well enough "a ancient hostelry / As any in the land may be . . . Now somewhat fallen to decay"—with the Red Horse still prancing on the sign (to alert drinkers, it is said, who could not read). The last Howe had died, and the building was "Alas, no longer an inn." He did see the clock and the Howe coat of arms he mentioned in the verses. "A man of ancient pedigree," the landlord tells the best known of the stories, "Paul Revere's Ride." He treasures the sword of his grandfather—short, ivory-handled—used by him "Down there at Concord in the fight." The success of the Wayside Tales prompted the change of the inn's name on its reopening; the successes of Henry Ford provided the means whereby it was twice restored and much enlarged. The cocktail napkins say Red Horse Room on them.

The daughter of Martha Bent Allen probably had no notion that she was directly descended from American Howes, in a straight line successive landlords of the inn from start to temporary finish.[24] As in the poem, these people claimed kinship with Sir William Howe (who is of genealogical interest as the illegitimate uncle of George III).

23. Samuel Longfellow, *Life of Henry W. Longfellow*, 2 vols. (Boston: Houghton Mifflin Co., 1886), 2:288. Longfellow's years are approximate.
24. David Wait Howe, *Howe Genealogies* (Boston: New England Historic Genealogical Society, 1929), 1–19, 40–41.

John How was born in Sudbury in 1640. His brother Samuel married an early Martha Bent, daughter of John and Martha Bent. They had a son David, who built a tavern in 1701 on land given him by his father. David's son Ezekiel put up the sign and was the officer "conspicuous at Concord." His son Adam, proprietor, was the father of Lyman, model for Longfellow's landlord, and a bachelor.

These facts jibe with Allen Bent's *The Bent Family in America.* Among the first settlers of Sudbury in 1638 were John Bent and his wife. They had two children there, a boy and a girl. The boy, Joseph, was the great-grandfather of Rufus Bent, father of Martha Bent, mother of Allan Melvill's daughter Ann. Joseph's sister, yet another Martha Bent, married the Howe who gave the land for the tavern.

When Paul Revere's news arrived, Lieutenant Colonel Ezekiel Howe and Sudbury minutemen marched to Concord and were directed to the Old North Bridge. There was a famous fracas about nine in the morning, with no great loss to either side. Ezekiel's sword apparently did hang over the tavern fireplace. Outside Sudbury, just off what is still the Boston Post Road, the inn appears on the map. One may dine here.

V

One last time, one more step. Martha Bent Allen (1777–1845) was the mother of Ann Middleton Allen (1798–1869), later Mrs. Nathaniel Tracy. Ann was named after her Scots grandmother, Ann Middleton (1741–1807). Martha Bent Allen had ten children and named the last Martha Allen (1818–92), after herself. As *her* daughter Anne would write, "on the twenty-sixth of February, 1840, Martha Allen of Newton married in the parlor of her aunt, Miss Ann Bent . . . at 216 Washington Street, Boston," William Gordon Means of Amherst, New Hampshire. Means became a successful manufacturer, moving from Manchester, New Hampshire, to Andover, Massachusetts, and Boston. He and Martha had eight children, six of whom survived.

One of these was Anne Middleton Means (1843–1923). She did not marry, but became the Means family genealogist and lived to see her *Amherst and Our Family Tree* (1921) in print. Anne and the other Means children were well known to Ann Tracy of Medford, Massachusetts, where she and Nathaniel Tracy retired in 1848. The town was five miles northwest of Boston and known for its countryside, with the Mystic River running through it. In retirement Tracy was a Senior Warden of Grace Episcopal Church. He died of cancer in 1866, his wife three years later of "paralysis."

She and Tracy had established a family plot at Mount Auburn Cemetery, a "Proper Boston Institution." And in the end, almost as though she'd had it in mind, she returned Bethuel Allen's kindness in placing her at the head of the list of his and Martha's children in his Bible. She put her mother's grave beside her with her stepfather's, where biological parents would go, and her husband and his first wife also next to her. She had married a man born, as Cervantes had it, with a silver spoon in his mouth. When the great fortune was gone, and Tracy without an heir anyway, she wrote a detailed will bequeathing over $32,000.[25] She left almost everything to Allens, including the "beautiful Tracy silver service."

Anne Middleton Means, the family historian, was schooled in Medford, then at Abbot Academy in Andover. As an adult she spent winters in Boston on Commonwealth Avenue and summers at Andover, where, it is said, her home was "a gathering place for young people." She belonged to Boston's Mayflower Club; a large part of her life centered on a new Trinity Church, where she was a communicant during "the inspiring ministry of Phillips Brooks," famed Episcopal bishop, renowned preacher, and author of "O Little Town of Bethlehem" (among many other works). For the rest she worked on the family tree, no small thing at 414 pages.

Thomas Melvill, as reported, regretted that Ann Middleton Allen had not been "brought up different." Perhaps he meant she had not grown up in a proper family. When he met her at thirty-four he probably saw a spinster's future writ plain in Ann Bent. He may have pitied childlessness, foreseen a lonely old age. Like his father and his brother Allan, Thomas was prolific.

25. It is worth remarking that Nathaniel Tracy's estate was valued at $14,000 when he died (Murray et al., "Allan Melvill's By-Blow," 6).

This is not how Anne Middleton Means in her *Family Tree* remembered "my mother's sister, for whom I was named."

> I must here . . . pay my tribute to Aunt Ann Tracy. . . . My mother was never strong and how she would have managed without the Family Providence in the shape of Aunt Ann, I do not know. Aunt Ann, who had no children of her own, had a way of swooping down upon our rapidly growing family whenever the need was greatest, and removing one or more of the "troublesome comforts" to her own home in Medford. She watched over us, mended our clothes or supplied us with new ones, and cared for us in every way. . . . I spent half my childhood with her.

Perhaps Ann M. Allen, or Tracy, brought up different like the Melvill brothers, might have ended as they did. Disasters.

2

Melvills, and the Heroine of *Pierre*

He suffers many maiden ladies with imagined pain. His Church is full of women who may not speak there, who may embroider little stools but must not presume to offer sacred paintings.

A. S. Byatt
Possession, 1990

I could wish there was a simple headstone for Priscilla.
Mrs. Herman Melville
Pittsfield, August 1, 1892

It is not as though Isabel, lovely orphaned heroine of Melville's *Pierre*, can be thought of as a real person. She is more like an illusion, emerging suddenly from a misty past all innocent of the world. She adores the improbable hero of the novel, her half-brother Pierre, as if unaware that her passion is banned. Pitying her, and feeling a need to expiate his father's sin, he throws up everything: estate, fiancée, family. He pretends to marry the girl, and moves her to the city. Soon he realizes that beneath his conscious desires lie others. All this is handled carefully; it is 1852. If details are taken literally, the passion is never consummated. But symbolism outweighs technicalities. The lovers are united, then kill themselves.

Melville would not have known that his book had a spiritual parent in the First American Novel, *The Power of Sympathy* (1789). Here as they are about to marry the lovers discover that like Pierre and Isabel they have the same father. Harriot falls ill and dies; Harrington, looking to Heaven where "our love will not be a crime," shoots himself. The wages of incest is death. In romance there is nowhere to go from there.

Isabel is out of romance. Such roots as she has in this world are shallow or obscure. Even so, the argument that she is based on an actual woman is better than forty years old and has not been upset. It is not claimed that she represents a Melville half-sister, though he is thought to have had one, and behind the mask of Pierre are his unmistakable features. Rather that the original was a first cousin, Priscilla by name. And if she should have a footnote as the model for Melville's only book-length heroine, it remains to be written, as does her story as a whole. Much has been learned in recent years about Priscilla's unusual parents and the family in which she lived until she was middle-aged[1]—people who have a story of their own. Still more recently, a number of letters she wrote nearly a century and a half ago began slowly coming to light. A sketchy picture is filling in. Finally, in her last years, an obscure nineteenth-century American comes into focus as a distinct if undistinguished woman who sat for the likeness, if it can be called that, the artist drew of her.

I

About all that used to be remembered of Thomas Melvill, Jr., was that he had "disgraced" himself by going broke in Paris and secretly marrying a Frenchwoman. He was the father of Priscilla and of several other Melvills; he was Herman Melville's favorite uncle, son of Major Thomas Melvill, Boston Patriot and Revolutionary War hero. (Herman's mother added the "e" to the name on her husband's early death; without it, the line traces anciently to the Melvills of Carnbee.)

---

1. Any account of Thomas Melvill must be heavily indebted to Stanton Garner, much the best-informed authority. See his "Picaresque Career of Thomas Melvill, Junior," *Melville Society Extracts* 60 (November 1984): 1–10, and ibid. (part 2), 62 (May 1985): 1, 4–10. Also informative are Merton M. Sealts, Jr., "Thomas Melvill, Jr., in *The History of Pittsfield*," *Harvard Library Bulletin* 35 (Spring 1987): 201–17, and "A Sheaf of Melville-Melvill Letters," *Harvard Library Bulletin* 35 (Summer 1987): 280–93. In addition, there is the late work done by Jay Leyda, cited below, note 5.

Gone to the Continent at nineteen Thomas Junior seems, on the whole, to have flourished abroad. He belonged to an American expatriate group that included James Monroe, the American minister, and Joel Barlow, who got rich trading in French government bonds while advancing a literary career. Young Melvill himself negotiated with Lord Malmesbury, emissary of William Pitt, and was once dispatched to Holwood House to deal directly with the Prime Minister on a matter of importance to Talleyrand.

In his nephew's view he thrived abroad until the end. Herman wrote a memoir of his uncle for a friend's history of Pittsfield, Massachusetts, where they had all lived (see Sealts, n. 1). In his short biography Thomas reminisces about France and "the stirring events that took place in that Country from the closing years of the Republic through the Consulate, and down . . . towards the collapse of the first Empire." His uncle had "found his way easy and delightful in the bright circles of the City on the Seine. . . . Many distinguished countrymen did he entertain at his table, together with Frenchmen of note. . . . I have frequently heard him name Lafayette." In 1802, the year of his marriage, his friend Barlow wrote President Jefferson from Paris to recommend Thomas for the Consulate there. Barlow praised moral character, talents, and republican principles, adding that Melvill had "established a banking and commercial house here, that is solid, and well conducted, deserving and enjoying an extensive credit" (Garner [1984], 5).

But Herman had not forgot another side of his uncle's financial life:

Of an enterprising & sanguine temper—too much so indeed— my uncle . . . engaged in various tempting ventures, incident to the wars then convulsing the Continent. Naturally he shared in many fluctuations.

I remember him telling me that . . . after prosperously closing in London some considerable affair, he held in his hands, before a cheery coal fire, the proceeds—negotiable bills, and for so large a sum that he said to himself—holding them at arms length—"This much is sure—here it is—the future is uncertain break off then and get the[e] back to

Boston Common.["] But a false friend—Hope by name . . .
advised to the contrary. (Sealts, 209)

Thomas had a friend named Recamier—apparently Jacques, a large
banker. His wife Julie was the storied Madame Recamier, whose
salon was the most famous in Paris. (David took her portrait, which
is prominent in the Louvre.) It was through this banker that Thomas
came to know the family of Pierre François Lamé-Fleury, particularly
a daughter who was a special favorite of M. Recamier. Her father
was a merchant from Nantes who had married Raymonde Françoise
Gavira of Cadiz. On June 29, 1802, according to the extant family
Bible, Thomas in Paris married their daughter, Françoise Marie des
Douleurs Eulogie Lamé-Fleury, born in Spain in 1781 (the groom
was five years older). Barlow is said to have been in attendance.
Spain had declared war on France in 1793, and Lamé-Fleury had
been deported to Nantes, where he was freed, and moved to Paris
(Garner 1984, 4). Herman had seen a miniature of the bride which,
he remarked, "presents a countenance of much beauty and of that
kind which forcibly arrests the attention" (Sealts, 210, photo). (Both
miniature and Bible were in the possession of Jean F. Melvill, who
descends from Thomas. She presented the portrait to the Berkshire
Athenaeum in 1987.) The countenance looks Mediterranean and very
fashionable.

Known as Fanny in this country, she wrote a letter in French to
her mother-in-law in Boston in 1805 (it survives at Harvard). In a
clear, unaffected hand she acknowledges a letter from her dear
mother written a few months earlier, and takes much pleasure in the
"ring containing your hair and those of my good father!!" It has been
long since she has written. "For more than a year I was constantly ill
and very sad." But now she is with dear Melvill and hopes her health
will improve after the "worries and sadness that I have felt for so
long." He too has had hardships but is well. "Our pretty little girl . . .
has never been sick . . . is always gay and good. . . . I embrace
tenderly my good father. Try to make him worry less about his son's
future. . . . Love always the one who cherishes and respects you,
your daughter

Paris the 16 August 1805

Fanny Melvill
[paraph]

She also remarked that she and "poor Melvill . . . drank (I like to think) the strongest dose of unhappiness" and trust that God will now favor them. But eventually, as Herman wrote in the memoir, "such reverses overtook" her husband that "recrossing the Ocean he returned to his father's roof. With him he brought . . . his wife & two young children."

By then it was 1811, and there were in fact four children: the pretty little Françoise, a son Thomas, another son Napoleon, called Allan, and Anne Marie Priscilla, who was born on November 5, 1810, and known as Priscilla, presumably after her Boston grandmother. Her father, now thirty-five, had been completely dependent on his father for a loan of perhaps $15,000 to get his family out of France and into the New World. War with England was again imminent. Thomas had friends from abroad in Washington, and so did his father, from Princeton days and Patriot Boston. He did not get a post there, but an appointment as Commissary of Subsistence, with the rank of Major, assigned to Pittsfield. General Henry Dearborn, a colleague of his father's at the Custom House in Boston, became a Major General based at Albany. To establish an army cantonment at Pittsfield in May 1812, Dearborn bought land there, and a cottage for the Superintendent and his family, to which a fifth child was born that year and named Henry Dearborn Melvill.

Fanny had been born and raised in Cadiz—founded by Phoenicians and known as a "clean white city with palm-lined promenades and parks" and a very old cathedral. Now thirty, she had for many years lived in fashionable Paris (that Barlow said was remarkable for "quantities of bare bubbies," with which Madame Recamier "made a great figure in London").[2] Pittsfield was different, although it did have a park, an open field in which two dirt roads converged at an elm. Facing the field were a church and perhaps twenty wooden shops and houses; other houses were on the roads to Lenox and Dalton. Outside town were a few mansions, notably the Van Schaack's. Near it was another early building, an inn. In time the Thomas Melvills would occupy the mansion and the Herman Melvilles

2. James Woodress, *A Yankee's Odyssey* . . . (Philadelphia: 1958), 226.

what had been the inn. But in 1812 Pittsfield was primitive and quiet. Suddenly it burst open.

Barracks were erected, local manufactures boomed. Thomas's commissary was the front. It provided a large "cash market for almost every variety of cloth, leather, iron, beef, pork, grain of all kinds, vegetables, hay, wood, wagons, horses, and whatever else."[3] Major Melvill, Jr., advertised "Cash, Cash, and a generous price, for cloths" in particular. To handle more purchasing, a deputy quartermaster was employed. Pittsfield was cordial to officers and soldiers both. From the start to the end of the war, officers of the post kept up "a round of balls which, if gallantry and beauty could make them so, were, beyond doubt, brilliant" (Smith, 315). The town was more "genial, merry, and unconstrained than at any period"—to the regret of "old people."

Nothing in the record provides a hint of how Fanny and five small children fared in this excitement. But local history could not be clearer on how things ended. The Berkshire Athenaeum in Pittsfield has today many handwritten sheets labeled " 'Corbin Manuscript Collection' in New England Historic Genealogical Society with Notes on Pittsfield Families. . . ." One short section is headed "Melville— Thomas" and reads:

> Sun [*The Pittsfield Sun*] of Apr. 14, 1814
> Died in this town on Friday the first of April Mrs. Fanny L'ame Fleury wife of Thomas Melville Jr. Esq. aged 32 years. She was a daughter of a distinguished family in Paris, a lady of eminent accomplishments and interesting virtues. During her short residence in the Country she attached to herself many dear friends who can, in some degree, estimate the loss sustained by her bereaved husband and young children. Firmly persuaded of the truth of the Christian religion, but observing the worship, which it enjoins, according to the Catholic forms she died in calmness and peace.

Herman wrote of his uncle that "his foreign wife paled and withered a transplanted flower." The last stanza of verses that follow the obituary begins similarly and ends in sorrow:

3. J.E.A. Smith, *History of Berkshire County* (New York: 1885), 2:309.

> Far from where bloomed her native rose
> And dearest kindred smiles,
> One grave protects in sweet repose
> The mother and her child's.

And so Peter Francis, Fanny's sixth child, was buried with her. He died, according to the family Bible, on April 11, "aged 25 days." And six days after that, Allan (Napoleon), born in France, died at six. In July the three bodies were transferred to "the Family Tomb, in the Burying Ground of Pittsfield" (Sealts, 207). Buried there as well, in 1821, was Françoise, the pretty little girl who was never sick. By this time Priscilla was eleven.

Thomas was a pious and apparently devout Episcopalian vestryman but, as his father reported,[4] Fanny on her deathbed had expressed "the wish that Priscilla be raised in her own faith." It would be twenty years before a Roman Catholic Mass was said in Pittsfield, and by the time St. Joseph's was built the Melvills had left town. Thomas had drunk, it would seem, a stronger "dose of unhappiness" than Fanny hoped for. But before long there was new hope. As commissary he had cleared, it is estimated, something like $30,000, and repaid the bulk of his father's loan. In the fall of 1815 the old Major paid a visit to Pittsfield with General Dearborn, who had a young and attractive granddaughter, Mary Ann Augusta Hobart. On the death of her parents she had become his ward. Little more than a month after the reunion with his father, Thomas and Mary wed. Twenty years younger than he, Mary was in Herman's eyes "an exemplary lady," and they became friends. She had, as well, exemplary ancestors, descending as she did from John Winthrop and Thomas Dudley, early governors of Massachusetts Bay Colony, founders and overseers of Harvard (Sealts, 206). In 1816 the old Major bought what had been the Van Schaack mansion (Herman would believe his uncle bought it), and, regrouped, the junior Melvills moved in. Thomas began reestablishing himself. He managed to get a fire engine purchased for the town, helped revive the local farming association,

---

4. William H. Gilman, *Melville's Early Life and "Redburn"* (New York: New York University Press, 1951), 70.

became president of it, and early won certificates for plowing, cultivation, and organization (ibid., 213). As a boy Herman farmed with him, and remembered the "laborious diaries" he kept of the farming.

But Thomas as a farmer proved a failure. Perhaps it was simply that, despite the fast start, he was just not cut out for it. For many years the Melvills lived a scrabbling existence at the great old place. After two decades at it, Thomas wrote Lemuel Shaw in early November that he feared the loss of his entire turnip crop—600 bushels—frozen in the ground.[5] What struck Herman was the incongruity of the scene: Thomas with his "mild and kindly" manners and a "faded brocade of old French breeding" as a dirt farmer. (He seemed the "shadowy aspect of a courtier of Louis XVI, reduced as a refugee to humble employment . . . far from the gilded Versailles" [Sealts, 214].) In 1822 he sent his tax bill for $59.86 to his father. "It is impossible," the old Major sputtered, "but that such a farm must pay its way & something be left, how is it that it does not?" (*The Melville Log Supplement*, 903). A "farmer *indebted*," the son replied, "can *but live*" (ibid., 904). Two years later it was "this is the last tax I ever will Pay (believe me)" (ibid., 905). (He once remarked of his son, "If he thinks at all, which I *very much* doubt . . .")[6]

There had been worse. In the spring of 1821 Thomas was "again imprisoned for debt" at Lenox.[7] This left his dependents, increased by the births of Robert in 1817, Mary Ann in 1818, and Julia Marie in 1820, fatherless and farmerless. (It was two days after he wrote from the Lenox jail that his first child, Françoise, died at seventeen.) On top of imprisonment were the effects of it, as he seems to have realized. In 1821 he wrote his brother Allan: "It is now eighty three days that I have been within these walls, that the sun has not shone on me—in that time I have not possessed *one Cent*, untill about ten days ago, I rec'd from my good father, ten Dollars towards paying my board." A month later his brother Allan, Herman's father, sent ten dollars. Thomas responded:

5. Jay Leyda, *The Melville Log with Supplement*, 2 vols. (New York: Gordian Press, 1969), 1:67.

6. Edwin H. Miller, *Melville* (New York: George Braziller, 1975), 59.

7. Jay Leyda, "From the *New Log*: The Year 1821," *Melville Society Extracts* 62 (May 1985): 3.

> I return herewith the Bill of the Columbia Bank, for ten dollars, contained in y^r aforesaid Letter—It being possible, that my 'Sensibility' has become 'morbid,' by four Months Seclusion in a space 18 by 12 feet. . . . I shall defer answering your Letter. (Leyda, *"New Log,* 1821," 3)

In 1835 he was back in the same place for the same reason.

Next year he had another opportunity. As Garner relates in detail, a man named Gear who had once farmed at Pittsfield returned to town. He was one who had gone west and prospered, having been a pioneer at Galena, Illinois, where a rich lode of lead had been struck. He bought a store there and, having lost his wife, he was looking for a mother to his children and a buyer for his farm. He found both and, remembering the polished Major from abroad at the cantonment— who was not thriving as a farmer—he offered him a position running a retail establishment in his store.

For some reason, "the Major"—as Gear called Thomas, who called Gear "Captain"—was indecisive, but in June 1837 he did head west with a son, John, twelve, a hard journey. In August he sent for the rest of his family; they had a wretched trip, crossing two rivers by canoe. At Galena things seemed to go better. Thomas was respected, thought an aristocrat, sometimes wore the grand outfit in which he was first married (Herman had seen it in the fields). Gears and Melvills became friendly, attended Episcopal services held in the courthouse. In 1840 the Major was elected secretary-treasurer of the Galena Chamber of Commerce. That summer, looking for a means of support in hard times, Herman visited with a friend. Thomas was now a notary public and ready to do business in real estate. But Herman was "anew struck by the contrast between the man and his environment" (Sealts, 215). Priscilla, still all but invisible at this distance, was now thirty.

There is disagreement about this period. Garner has it that when Herman was in town Thomas was "at the peak of his Galena prosperity" (part 2:6). Thirty years ago G. Thomas Tanselle had not seen it that way.[8] He thought that Herman had found his relatives "in

8. In "Herman Melville's Visit to Galena in 1840," *Journal of the Illinois State Historical Society* 53 (Winter 1960): 376–84.

worse financial condition than they had been back at Pittsfield" (nothing was financially worse than debtor's prison). But Tanselle heard in Galena that the Major had been a liability to Gear, and "did not improve his position by moving west" (Tanselle, 383). He was told, further, that Melvill had been mixed up in some scandal, was ordered out of town, and was separated from his wife. Anyway, "something was strange about his position" (ibid., 384).

Garner appears to explain a lot of this (part 2:8) with the help of Gear's daughter Clarissa's "Autobiography. . . ."[9] She remembered Thomas as an older gentleman, an aristocratic son of "old blue blood Yankees," once minister to France, who married into French nobility. (His second wife came from "one of the highest families" in Massachusetts.) She recalled the satin and gold-laced wedding clothes. Her father reported that at Pittsfield the Major had spent most of his and his new wife's money.

The trouble at Galena probably came to a head in the summer of 1841. (Garner says the date is "far from certain" but fits other evidence.) Clarissa got the story from her stepmother, an eyewitness to the scene. Thomas had a pleasant home, she writes; the family were "lovely people," he had "every luxury." But at the store he had "too much money to handle." Clerks whispered that he was embezzling; word reached the Gears. Confronted with the charge, Thomas confessed and begged mercy. The money (a "vast sum," she says) was gone. Gear said he could put Melvill in jail for life, but for the sake of his gray hair and family would not punish him—just never wanted to see him again.

Clarissa Hobbs sounds credible, but not everyone accepts her, the sole source of the story. She says she was "too young"—eleven—to hear what was said "upstairs." Indeed she admits she did not hear until "years after I was grown," which could have been a long time after the event. She adds that Thomas did not live "more than a year" after his exposure, which is not so. If he had "every luxury," it is odd that Herman did not detect the contrast with Pittsfield poverty—or any prospect of a job in the area (which is known to have

9. "Autobiography of Clarissa Emely Gear Hobbs," *Journal of the Illinois State Historical Society* 17 (1925): 611–714.

been seriously depressed at the time). Indeed Thomas, though employed at Gear's, seems to have been scrambling for a living—advertising in 1840 his services in practically any line of business, including the collection of debts (Garner, 2:6). On the other hand, if his disgrace was so open that clerks were talking, it is hard to account for his being given a position of trust in the U.S. Lead Mines in 1843 (ibid., 2:8). But if there was no large scandal, what was the source of rumors Tanselle heard as late as 1960? A month after her husband's death in 1845, Mary Ann (who does not sound at all "separated") wrote Shaw that it was "at great sacrifice of personal feeling" that she was going to leave Galena and return to Pittsfield (*The Melville Log*, 1:198). Evidently her memories of that place were more disturbing than anything she had survived in Illinois.

The family did return to Pittsfield, where they were living in 1850 in the great house on the farm when the Herman Melvilles came for the summer to board. Mary Ann gave her nephew a copy, signed "Aunt Mary," of Hawthorne's *Mosses from an Old Manse*, which triggered an historic essay and friendship. But the place could not be made to pay, and was sold in 1852. Mary went back to Galena—with all her children, she wrote, except Priscilla, who was in Canandaigua, New York (Sealts, 281). Still handsome in her age, Mary Melvill died in 1884. The good Galena house was in Melvill hands until 1916.

Why Priscilla was in the Finger Lakes region of upstate New York raises the question of what became of the other surviving children born to Fanny Melvill and raised in the rural Berkshires. Two others were living. The youngest, Henry Dearborn, has been described as "insane" (*The Melville Log*, 1:397). But he was not, according to his father, "strictly speaking *non compos*. . . . [A]s to dates . . . he is particularly retentive; —Has never been able to write or Cypher," perhaps because of "early paralysis of his right side—He is fond of reading entertaining subjects, but the recollection of them, is soon obliterated" (*Log Supplement*, 911). Thomas was asking Judge Shaw if Henry were "*legally capable* to affix his mark to a public act." The question was of interest: his mother had left her children some "French property" or funds; only he and Priscilla lived long enough to receive any.

Best hope for Thomas among Fanny's children was his namesake

Thomas Wilson, born in Paris in 1806 and formally named Pierre. In 1826 he was appointed Midshipman in the U.S. Navy (*Log*, 1:23). Before long he hoped to pass his examination without going back to sea. But he did return, and two years later was suspended from duty for jumping with his feet on the chest of a sailor (*Log*, 1:38, 49). In 1832 he had a severe case of Asiatic Cholera and intended to return to Pittsfield. ("Pity that he had not . . . sooner," remarked Gansevoort, Herman's brother, "for he has almost broken his father's heart" [*Log*, 1:55].) Finally his father had a letter from his son ("the first since about 9 yrs") (*Log*, 1:121). Three years later Robert wrote that his half-brother had "left off his habit of drinking" (ibid.). But later in 1844 *The Friend of Temperance and Seamen* reported the death of "Thos. W. Malvill, belonging to Boston, Mass. His remains were brought to Lahaina, and interred on shore" (*Log*, 1:184). Shaw later learned the cause of death, "inflammatory Rheumatism & Scurvy." Ship's Captain asked if he had "any message for his friends, he answered no, the few clothes he had which were very poor he gave the crew" (*Log Supplement*, 913).

And then there was Priscilla.

II

Paris-born Anne Marie Priscilla Melvill wrote several letters during the period 1848–53 to her cousin Augusta Melville, Herman's sister. They were stored in some trunks found in 1983 in a barn at Gansevoort, New York, at the house of her late uncle Herman Gansevoort, where she had been living until shortly before her death in 1876. (They are now in the New York Public Library, where a few others have long rested in the Gansevoort-Lansing Collection. Some of Priscilla's letters are also in the Shaw Collection at the Massachusetts Historical Society. Hershel Parker, editor (with Jay Leyda) of *The New Melville Log*, in progress, generously transcribed a few for the present writer.) Apparently the earliest mention of Priscilla yet to surface, however, is dated March 1824 (she was thirteen). From New York Herman's mother wrote that it had been a "Winter of sickness & Gloom to me, Priscilla has kept to her room on the Third Story nearly three months" (*Log*, 1:17). She was living with the Allan Melvills on Cortland Street. The privy out back was condemned (Gilman, 27), and they were about to move to a two-story brick house in "the region of good air [&] good water" at suburban Bleecker Street.

But as Parker has observed, [10] Priscilla really began to emerge in a few letters from Pittsfield to Augusta in New York written by her younger half-sister Julia Maria Melvill, born in 1820, daughter of Thomas and Mary Ann. (Julia is negligent with dates; she writes from Pittsfield until otherwise noted.) Snippings sketch the story.

> March 1834   Pittsfield has been very dull . . . everyone is getting married but Priss . . .

> March 1834   . . . in my short life the Cholera Summer was the pleasantest because my beloved brother [Allan] was here and now he is numbered with the dead . . .

> Sept Friday 1834   Priss says if you don't love her she loves you but it is time to turn in now.

> Wednesday 26 1834   You may hear of a *weding* before long it is Prises only think of that . . . I expect she will be drest in the tip of the mode . . .

> March 4 1835   . . . give my love to my 1000 cousins . . .

> [1835?]   . . . the man over in the east street has not been here yet but Pris expects him Sunday night.

> March 1837   . . . I cannot think for Priss is teaching Gans to sing & of all the noises I ever . . .

> June. Sunday 1837   . . . Papa is on the way up the Missippi now I suppose. . . . Herman . . . is very good very polite. . . . We will try not to make him quite a savage while he resides in the country as you fear . . . to Galena next spring . . .

10. Hershel Parker, "The *New Melville Log*: A Progress Report and an Appeal," *Modern Language Studies* 20 (Winter 1990): 53–66.

Priscilla is coming home tomorrow it is quite a Jubille to have her here once in a while . . .

Sept 5th 1837   Ma heard from father . . . he was well John wrote a few lines givin a description of the country. He says the place abounds in poisonous snakes.

Thursday Nov 22, 1837 . . . write me when Herman returns and burn this . . . no letter from pa for a week . . . I hope that he will send for us early next spring . . . an age since I saw him

April 17th . . . father has not determined if he will remove to Galena or stay here . . . much pleasanter to go than to remain here vegetating

April 17 1838   Priss will be home in a few days. Mr Dodge is going to leave that school and the gentleman that is to take it is not going to allow any parties, or any gentlemen to visit the young ladies and he is going to have a wall six foot high built before the house, it will be a complete nunnery. . . .

August 1838 . . . we intend to turn our faces to the "Far West" on the 16th of September . . . Pittsfield is as good a place as I wish to live in. . . . Pa wrote that this was the time.

Cleveland Thursday 1838 . . . arrived at Pittsburg . . . very dirty and smokey . . . heartily sick of this horrid traveling. . . . Tomorrow we expect to be seasick.

A report on the Galena Melvills, written by the Reverend Edward Ballard, their Pittsfield minister, on September 4, 1841:

Robert wishes me to add that his father is a man of broken constitution, and his mother but the shadow of what she was: and that Julia, by reason of sickness is nearly blind, though he hopes not permanently so. Calamity appears to be the lot of that family. (*Log*, 1:120)

But Julia wrote Augusta from Galena three times:

June 27 1842   Pa, ma, and all the family are well. . . .
George is a clerk in a bookstore . . . Allan spends most of his
time in pa's office . . . a good view of the steamboats.

June 29 1842   We hear quite accidentally that Herman has
gone to sea. . . . I was cut out for an old maid

July 30 1842   . . . Miss Julia M. Melvill Spinster. Galena
Illinois.

By now Julia's older brother was trying to make a go of the farm
back at Pittsfield. Then a letter from Priscilla herself at Pittsfield, to
Lemuel Shaw, dated July 22, 1846:

My brother Robert sent me an affectionate invitation to
share his home & labors—which I joyfully & thankfully accepted—so I arrived here towards the last of May—I left the
[Galena] family well, excepting Julia, & we *fear* that *she*, poor
Girl, is in a consumption. *(The Melville Log Supplement,* 916)

Julia was very likely in a consumption; she had died four days back,
not having lived long enough to be an old maid.

At first, Priscilla comes into somewhat giddy view. In August 1847
in New York City Herman had married Elizabeth Shaw, daughter of
Lemuel Shaw, his father's best friend. Next month his brother Allan
married Sophia Thurston. Then Priscilla in Pittsfield wrote the men's
sister Augusta that

Allan & Sophia left *New York* for a short time—for space &
freedom to enjoy the dawn of their wedded bliss—was their
love as ethereal (like Herman's & Lizzie's) that it bore them
upward, toward a heavenly Paradise—or did they seek one
among the lovely beauties of earth? *(Log,* 1:260)

Sometime in the same month she wrote Augusta a curious letter of
love and death:

. . . will you not cast the broad mantle of charity over this
piece of *seeming* neglect—and take me to your heart again,

as on *certain* freezing mornings that are within the memory of both of us—when I was wont to be encircl'd in *those graceful* arms of yours, tighten'd by the chords of affection (& SOMETHING else—that I will not name *even* on paper) untill I could fancy myself clasped in the *cold* embrace which we poor mortals think of with dread—perhaps you are shocked and besides, must think it strange that I feel a desire, to revive sensations that cause a shudder through the shrinking frame—But my pen is running wild tonight—& I must not allow it to be so unmanageable. (Gansevoort-Lansing, New York Public Library [NYPL])

It is at this point that letters from Priscilla to Augusta, newly come to light at Gansevoort, enter the correspondence:

Pittsfield April 3rd '48
Dear Cousin 'Gus'—
    I had . . . almost despaired of hearing from any of you again—however, your sweet letter brought joy to my heart when *at* LAST it came. . . . [Y]ou KNOW the magic power you possess, & exercise, in a most arbitrary way, by *manner, tongue,* & *pen* over the yielding wills of your passive victims. . . . But *we* had attributed your silence to something entirely different . . . confirmed in the belief that you felt . . . by a residence & GREAT establishment in New York far above the condition of your country cousins, & had concluded to forget them—but we know that the return of summer would certainly bring you to your senses, & to Pittsfield. . . . I believe that Herman has been disappointed in his plans for passing the time during his short stay with us—especially since he has manifested so much constancy toward the object of his *first love* . . . Berkshire farm—as to tear himself from the idol of his heart. . . . [H]e can inform you that Robert is making preparations for opening his house for a large family during the summer months—& I hope he may succeed in making it profitable & furthermore, he has paid me a visit in my adopted home in the village—& can testify that my situation is a very

pleasant one . . . accept my sincere love—*for my dearly beloved cousin Augusta*— Priscilla. (Augusta Papers, NYPL)

Pittsfield   June 15 [1848], Priscilla to Lemuel Shaw
. . . it has become necessary for me to provide myself *immediately* with a little *extra* outfit—please don't open your eyes so wide, Sir, It is *not* for a *wedding*—but Mr & Mrs Tyler, in whose family I have been since I returned from Boston are about resigning their present situation as principals of *this* school for Boys . . . & will remove directly to Canandaigua to preside over a flourishing Female seminary & are desirous that I should accompany them. (*The Melville Log Supplement*, 919)

Canandaigua   August 20 1848   Priscilla to Augusta[?]
Do any of the Melville tribe, residing in the "city of Gotham"—remember a certain cousin "Priss" of theirs . . . This circular will inform them of her where-a-abouts . . . she has *again* deserted the home of her early days . . . (Augusta Papers, NYPL)

August 28 1848   Priscilla to Augusta, continued
. . . We are so busily occupied in making arrangements for the commencement of this term. . . . I hope that my aunties & cousins retain sufficient interest . . . my situation . . . continues to be a good home with Mr & Mrs Tyler . . . a beautiful home in this lovely village . . . surrounded with shrubbery & gravel walks . . . & an abundance of fruit. . . . I presume the Longfellows [poet and family] are still there . . . much love . . .   Cousin "Priss"

[Printed enclosure]

ONTARIO FEMALE SEMINARY
Canandaigua, N.Y.
. . . happy to announce its continuance under the care of EDWARD G. TYLER, A. M. and lady, recently Associate Principals of the Young Ladies' [sic] Institute, Pittsfield, Mass. . . .
. . . personal supervision of the pupils will devolve entirely

upon Mrs. Tyler and her female assistants. . . . Pupils from abroad will be received into the family of the Principal, where they will enjoy the attentions and safeguards of home, and will be expected to conform to the proprieties of life . . . well-regulated families . . . refined society. (Augusta Papers, NYPL)

Canandaigua December 30 [1850]   Priscilla to Augusta
. . . I am smitten with nothing more loathesome than *chilblains*. [T]ell me how you pass the time at this unlovely season of the year. . . . (Augusta Papers, NYPL)

January 28th—1850   Priscilla to Augusta
. . . your letters like "angel's visits"—I wait very patiently. . . . [Y]ou see I write from Pittsfield . . . my Mother & Brothers & Sisters here. . . .
I am indeed a pilgrim . . . having "no continuing city." I cannot say at present whether I shall remain *here*, or return to Canandaigua—my duties there were very fatiguing—& confin'd me too closely . . . must have made a *frightful* alteration in my appearance. . . . It seems to give my friends & acquaintances *pain*, rather than pleasure to meet me after an absence of eighteen months—& they almost shrink . . . exclaiming how miserable you look . . . I have about determin'd to spare . . . secluding myself entirely or leaving for a strange land. . . . I believe I must return to Canandaigua in self-defense—I do not *feel* as bad as I *look* perhaps—enough concerning the frail tabernacle of the flesh . . .
We have all been very much interested in "Redburn"s voyage . . . fascinating . . . I see that Herman has perhaps already return'd from Europe. . . . [O]ur school numbers 195 pupils—72 of whom are boarders— (Augusta Papers, NYPL)

Canandaigua February 28th '50
. . . alas—*here I am*
. . . it requires all the powers of pleasing, to charm away the *hysterics* . . . in a family made up of so many sensitive

young girls. . . . *[S]ympathy could not* be *misplaced,* upon *me*
. . . (Augusta Papers, NYPL)

Ontario Female Seminary October 7th '52
. . . I *am* becoming *heartily* tir'd of my present situation
. . . & would be greatly obliged to any good angel, whose
vision can penetrate the future . . . I often dream of blissful
solitude—freedom from care—& a *crust* & *water,* in the
"Brown Cottage"—which quiet retreat from . . . the vexations
& anxieties of life . . . 'Gus' dear . . . I presume a little . . .
& request you to act as my man of business in this matter—
merely for the present to make some CARELESS inquiries as
to the *terms* that the present proprietress would be willing to
dispose of her coveted property . . . to posses[s] the little
paradise—& rent it—until I finally conclude to sacrifice my
present enjoyment of abundance & the accompanying respon-
sibilities—perhaps—again I could bargain with a respectable
family to furnish two of the rooms myself & *board* for the
rest—Tell me . . . & will you take all this trouble for me? —
But mind—be very ⌐autious—& do not appear too *anxious* to
purchase—But if the good lady only demands a *moderate*
sum—the equivalent can be given in exchange with very little
delay—Our mutual friend Mr Cole would willingly counsel us
in the affair. . . . (Augusta Papers, NYPL)

Ontario Female Seminary November 1st '52
. . . You make a *sober* reality—indeed—of my pleasant
romance connected with the "Brown" cottage—& your affectionate solicitude for my greatest happiness has penetrated
deep into the SHADOWS . . . & discovers a grim array of
frightful spectres, enough to daunt the courage of any *helpless*
woman . . . & the closest *calculation* would not make my
little income suffice, & my timid spirit sacrificed . . . the
favorite scheme that imagination had cherished.
　—I appreciate the affection that presided at Arrow-head
about the matter. . . . My dearest coz—*never* fear at my
"*misconstruing*" your motives, in placing the *darker* shades of
the picture before me. . . . I am resolved to improve the very

first opportunity that presents itself for bettering my condition. . . . [I]t is very rarely, *one*, in the station to which by birth & tastes I feel myself to belong—is cast upon this world, to depend upon their own exertions. . . . It is *more this* circumstances of *birth* & *tastes* that causes my spirit to chafe *thus* . . . & doubtless I should consider my lot a most enviable one—did not my native aristocracy rebel. . . . I *would* like very much to find constant employment for my needle—in that case I *could hoard* as you suggest—If *not*—I can drag along an existence *here* . . . my wild dream is ended, for the present— (Augusta Papers, NYPL)

Seminary—March 21 53
. . . you owe me a letter, since time immemorial. . . . Mr Tyler my friend & patron, will be in Pittsfield next week . . . & he would feel *much* gratified, I know, by receiving a called from *Herman*. (Augusta Papers, NYPL)

Ontario Female Seminary May 23rd '53
dear Gus—can you by any artifice procure me Herman's autograph—*send it*, & say *nothing* to him
. . . more concerned that the crust of selfishness is gathering . . . with the rapid approach of age . . . this lamentable & almost *inevitable* consequence of the single state—indeed—poor solitary woman, after the attractive season of youth is past, is . . . sure to become the victim of its hardening influences—imagining that she is not properly appreciated.
. . . cherished memories of our earlier years . . . your frequent allusions to those happy times . . . hallow'd among your most cherish'd recollections.
. . . my burden is becoming *too* oppressive—& I am about decided on resigning my *present* post.
When will the "Isle of the Cross" [novel HM was "prevented" from publishing] make its appearance? I am constantly looking for notices of it. (Augusta Papers, NYPL)

Ontario Female Seminary June 12th '53

. . . affectionate invitation . . . from the depths of *your* warm heart . . . to visit "Arrow-head," if possible—at an early day . . . I must resign these cares . . . endeavoring to procure board & a room . . . at the *cheapest possible* rate, in the village—& peace out a living with my needle. . . . I would greatly prefer it to going into a family—in any capacity—I have had trial of *that*. . . . I shall soon be a waif on the sea of fate—I am glad to hear such a favorable report of Lizzie—she is really gathering quite a little family around her . . . the "Isle of the Cross" is almost a twin sister of this little one & I think should be nam'd for the heroine—if there *is* such a personage. . . . Many thanks for the autograph. (Augusta Papers, NYPL)

Twenty fourth Street [New York]—Tuesday Morn^g

Allan & Sophia are completing their morning toilet. . . . We arrived in N'York about 9 o' clock—found them awaiting us with a hearty welcome. . . .

Thursday Morn^g

. . . cousin Tom proposed our going to the "Palace" . . . I was wearied with admiring the *place*.

Saturday Eve^g February [?]

. . . Mrs Thurston took *me* with *her* down Broadway . . . a charming promenade. . . . She took me to an embroidery store & bought me a pretty stamped collar. . . . Dear Dutti— . . . My best love to Lizzie & Herman, & kiss the children for *"Tousin Cilla"* . . . (Augusta Papers, NYPL)

[Pittsfield] March 27, 1854   Priscilla to Lemuel Shaw

We—that is—Lizzie, Augusta, Herman, the little folks, & myself are driven to the necessity of being *very* amiable and *obliged* to play the agreeable for mutual entertainment *within* doors—for the weather continues very severe, gales, and snow storms prevail, *even yet*, with *no* promise of spring—and we are all becoming rather weary of winter quarters—But we are all in the enjoyment of very robust health. (*Log*, 1:486)

Priscilla's "little income" is explained by a letter, contributed by Hershel Parker and marked "uncorrected," in the Shaw Papers at the Massachusetts Historical Society:

> Galena   April 24, 1841   Thomas Melvill Jr. to Lemuel Shaw
> . . . Once, while sick, I wrote you particularly in respect to the legacy of M Lamé Duperon [?], of Orleans, (in France) which by the death thru [?] paternal grandfather, & g⁴mother—(*M Lamé Fleury*) has fallen to Thᵒ, Priscilla, & Henry—and which it seems, was inscribed on the *"Grand livre,"* of the public debt of France, in *"Rentes"* [income], that is to say, the annual interest at 5%. . . .

(This was the bequest Priscilla would profit from. Henry probably did too, since she will refer to "my share.")

Parker also supplied this from the Shaw Papers:

> Galena March 31 1853 Priscilla Melville [*sic*] to Lemuel Shaw
> Again I address you my annual request . . . that if convenient, Sir, you will forward my share of interest money, in the form of a *draft* . . . & direct to the care of Mr. E. G. Tyler . . . I am not in particular need of the money, if it *accumulates* by being left from year to year. Will you please inform me if *this is so? . . . I should feel rich, if I could make my little means suffice to board,* & supply my necessary wants.
> Mr Tyler has $875 of mine, at 7 per cent interest.
> *My* share of the money that was paid for *that town lot* in Pittsfield
> *Robert got possession* of, & I will probably *never* shall see it. . . .

(A document at the Berkshire Athenaeum, Pittsfield, dated 1853—courtesy again of Parker—shows Priscilla owning "1/2 of 13/16 Lot $200.00" and owing $12.00 in taxes.)

On February 15, 1855, came the anticipated announcement, a running advertisement in *The Pittsfield Sun:*

[pointed finger] Miss Melville will devote herself to EMBROI-
DERY and the making of the nicer articles pertaining to
Ladies', Gentlemen's, or Children's wardrobes—at her room,
opposite the Methodist Church in Fenn Street, up stairs.
(*Log*, 2:488)

Priscilla wrote Shaw on the following October 24th that "Herman
called to see me this afternoon—left *all well* at home—Augusta was
preparing to attend a great party, this Eveᵍ. . . ." (*Log*, 2:509)

It may be fitting that presently available Priscilla letters run out
with a great party to which she would not be invited. Larger things
were running out. In New York on October 3, 1858, Sophia Melville,
who had wed Allan, died at thirty (*Log*, 2:595). And on October 22,
among the advertisements in the *Berkshire County Eagle*, a column
headed DIED began:

In the town, Oct. 20th, Miss Priscilla Melville, aged 54,
daughter of the late Major Thomas Melville.

Six days later the *Sun* said the same. Actually she was just short of
forty-eight. The Immediate Cause of Death, according to the City
Clerk for the City of Pittsfield, was "Consumption." Several Melvills
died of that.

III

The idea that Priscilla was a "sufficient model" for Isabel in *Pierre*
was originally Henry A. Murray's. He devoted a page (lxv) to it in his
landmark introduction to the Hendricks House Edition (1949) of the
novel. Most of his succinct reasons for the notion have held up over
the years, but seem not to have been developed at all—or added to.
A couple that seem weak may perhaps be replaced with new ones.
Until recently, a great deal of Priscilla was hidden in the Gansevoort
barn and is still generally unavailable. But much had long been known,
and with basic parallels Murray was on target.

Isabel and Priscilla were born in France to "French" ladies. Both sailed to America as infants. Both were very young when they lost their mothers. As an orphan in America, Isabel lived in several country houses when little—as Priscilla may have done when her father had both children and farm to look after. Isabel lived for a time in what was clearly a place for the insane; if Henry ever suffered from any mental disorder, Priscilla may have had some memory of it. Isabel inherited her mother's dark beauty; so perhaps did Priscilla. Isabel had memories of coffins moving in and out of her house; so very likely did Priscilla, who was four years old when three in the family died. Isabel once had two languages; Priscilla's parents spoke French before she would have learned English. Both girls had clear memories of a gentleman who is plainly based on Herman's father, who (as Murray suspected in 1949) had an illegitimate daughter. Both women have an older brother named Pierre. And Herman may have thought of Priscilla as much like a sister when she lived in New York with his family while he was young.

The two women match in other ways. Isabel was never a schoolteacher, but, as far as is known, neither was Priscilla. Since she lived at a school in Canandaigua it is said that she taught there,[11] but she never achieved such status. The Ontario Female Seminary Winter 1849–50 Catalogue lists the faculty by name; she was not on it. "PRISCILLA MELVILLE, f, 38, born Mass." is entered in the Canandaigua Federal Census of 1850, but although one man at the school is identified as "Labour" and one woman as "Waitress," there is a blank for Priscilla under "Occupation."[12] (Very likely she was among the female assistants to Mrs. Tyler in monitoring the proprieties of refined society, which would have ruled out hysterics.)

A talent that Priscilla did have in common with Isabel seems not to have been mentioned. She became an embroiderer. The first time Pierre thinks of the beautiful, exotic heroine is in a very odd way: as "the sewing girl" in "a memorable scene in the sewing-circle at the Miss Pennies."[13] Isabel underlines this by repeating it. She had

11. Sealts, "A Sheaf of Melville-Melvill Letters," 281.
12. Thanks to Melville J. Boucher of Canandaigua, direct descendant of Thomas Melvill by his second wife, for information on the Seminary.
13. *Pierre; or, The Ambiguities*, ed. Harrison Hayford, Hershel Parker, and G. Thomas

shrieked and fainted at the sound of the hero's name. Evidently Priscilla was known for her skill before she set up shop in Fenn Street; Mrs. Thurston, Allan Melville's mother-in-law, bought her a piece of embroidery on Broadway.

Murray writes that Priscilla's "feelings and thoughts" were, like Isabel's, "vague and confused, mysteriously dream-like." He must have been judging from the few letters available to him, perhaps from the unique one of 1847 to Augusta in which the shudder of death interrupts a tight embrace. This was available to Murray though he never mentions it. It is not at all vague, is not so much confused as incoherent, and is more like nightmare than dream. William Gilman, who finished his book before reading Murray's, prints the 1847 document (69) and describes it as "warm with memories of pleasures the Melvill cousins had enjoyed together" as if they were joys of berry-picking and sleigh rides. But then he reverses himself, remarking that in this letter Priscilla "reveals a romantic and passionate nature from which Melville may have borrowed the incandescent ardor" of Isabel. He suggests as well that the "dynamic" Priscilla "derived intense passions" from her "French and Spanish mother" (67), though elsewhere she does not seem especially dynamic or ardent. The telling point seems to be that Isabel's passion for her brother is like Priscilla's for her cousin in that the thought or excitement of death quickly overcomes earthly desire, and both succumb to it: Priscilla wants to relive sensations of death's embrace, and Isabel takes poison. (The spirit of Romanticism, perhaps.)

Hershel Parker has a good ear, remarking of Priscilla's letters that at times her "voice" sounds like Isabel's.[14] Neither voice is described, but Isabel's is extravagant and overblown, Priscilla's overstated, hyperbolic. Both express sexuality. Isabel: "my brother . . . thou hast that heavenly magnet in thee, which draws all my soul's interior to thee" (157). "I am too full without discharge" (113). Rhetoric can carry her away: "my brother . . . art thou an angel, that thou canst overleap all the heartless usages and fashions of a banded world . . . if thou yieldest to that heavenly impulse which alone can lead thee to

Tanselle (Evanston and Chicago: Northwestern University Press and The Newberry Library, 1971), 145.

14. Parker, "The *New Melville Log*," 63.

respond to the . . . unquenchable yearnings of my bursting heart?
. . . behold how I rave" (64). (Priscilla: "my pen is running wild.")
"Pierre . . . I must work for thee! See, I will sell this hair; have
these teeth pulled out" (333).

Of course Isabel is on the verge of madness. But Priscilla has her
own flights. Wedded bliss lifting lovers toward Heaven and so forth,
Augusta's power over yielding victims, her own appearance so frightful that she thinks of foreign parts; dreams of a cottage, a crust, and
water; is a helpless waif. (She does not seem at all religious, nor
does Isabel.)

But it is in sudden moments of recognition that the seed of the
heroine becomes visible in the cousin. Portraits play a large role in
the novel. First, the two of Pierre's father, easily recognized pictures
of Allan Melvill (one now in the Metropolitan Museum, the other in
the Huntington Art Gallery). Later, as if to underline the sexual
theme, the young couple visit a famous painting of Beatrice Cenci,
the nineteenth century's classic victim of incest (though Isabel is no
victim).

No matter. It is another portrait that displays the heroine's origin
in life. It appears at the heart of the first part of Isabel's story as told
to Pierre and the reader (124). When a girl she had lived in a
farmhouse where a pleasant woman taught her to sew. The gentleman drawn from Melville's father begins to call on her. One unforget-
table day, while looking into calm water, Isabel is seized with the
likeness of her face to this kind man's.

The incident gives fictional life to a fact. Herman would have known
from his uncle Thomas, who encountered his brother's secret daughter in Boston, that her face was "biological confirmation" of Allan's
paternity. This is why Chief Justice Lemuel Shaw, friend to all
Melvilles and Melvills, who had also just met the woman, was so
disturbed that Allan's father, the old Major, still living in Boston,
might also see her.[15] (His wife had.) He would then have spotted the
truth: his flawless son (as opposed to Thomas) had an unacknowl-
edged child. It would have crushed the old man as it did young

15. See Henry A. Murray et al., "Allan Melvill's By-Blow," *Melville Society Extracts* 61
(February 1985): 2.

Herman, who passed the blow along to Pierre who is wrecked by it. After Isabel sees her reflection, the gentleman whispers "Father" to her (124). But "at the last he came not at all . . . they said *Dead* to me." And "the former money was now gone." Exactly as when Allan suddenly died bankrupt.

After identifying himself to Isabel the gentleman, looking at her anew, is "astonished, confounded": he "looked at me, then at a very little round picture . . . which he took from his pocket, and yet concealed from me" (124). It is of course her mother; her father is now shaken by the powerful resemblance to the daughter. The woman in the picture is of course Françoise Lamé-Fleury. The man has what Herman called the "miniature I have seen of her" (it is round). Fanny had only one daughter, Priscilla, whom Herman could have known, the other having died when he was two. Jean F. Melvill inherited and gave away a rare little painting—of a real-life mother of an unreal fictional character. Priscilla is not a "sufficient model" for Isabel; as only living daughter of the same woman, Priscilla was Isabel in the flesh.

IV

Herman lived until 1891. For the next two years his widow was in touch with Helen Jean Melvill of Galena, Thomas's last daughter, who lived in the old house until 1905. Lizzie was in Pittsfield when she wrote. Priscilla was buried in the new Pittsfield Cemetery, where Lot 18, Hope Mount, had been conveyed to Mary Ann Melvill in 1851. For a long time Priscilla was the only one buried in it.

Lizzie wrote Helen Jean: "Please address me Mrs. Herman M— our carrier is used to that." On August 1, 1892, she told Helen that a hedge her husband had planted at Arrowhead (she did not note that it was his birthday) was "a stately row of tall and beautiful trees . . . it is nearly 30 [years] since I lived here . . . and the little house in Fenn st where Priscilla passed her last days looks exactly the same— And I have been to the cemetery which has grown to be as lovely a resting place as I have ever seen . . . but the Melvill lot . . . weedy and neglected. . . . I once planted a willow over Priscilla's mound, but it died out" (Sealts, 285). Next year she wrote again. "I saw Mr. McArthur and expressed my approval at the appearance of the cemetery lot—he did not make the mound over Priscilla's grave because it was so obliterated that he did not know exactly where it was" (291). She planned for a stone with all the initials on it (A M P M, as she wrote), but it never came to be.

On a fall day at Arrowhead the plowed field north of the farmhouse that yielded the eponymous Indian relics now appears just as it must have in 1850 when Herman found them. In Canandaigua, on the other hand, the handsome Ontario Seminary buildings and grounds have been erased for a massive intersection of highways. The little house in Fenn Street was razed for the large white-pillared Pittsfield City Hall; the Methodist Church has been completely rebuilt. At Hope Mount there is a marble gravestone reading MELVILL. in embossed letters, resting on a thick heavily mossed pediment stone. It is the only stone in the lot, though Henry Melvill died in 1896 at eighty-four and is buried here somewhere. When last visited the ground was covered with October leaves.

For Priscilla the revels never began, but she melted into thin air anyhow, and left scarce a rack behind. Some letters that still have life. But no likeness save Isabel, and that in words. No descendents; until the very last no Occupation. No ring of hairs, no knowing where Lizzie planted the willow. But no embroidery, not a scrap? Jean F. Melvill writes that she has not heard of any,[16] "although there is just one possibility—a piece of needlepoint that was used for a seat cover on one of the Chippendale-style chairs that belonged to my great grandfather," who was Thomas. This might have been Priscilla's work—she just doesn't know.

From this perspective it seems rather more than a possibility. In any event, Jean Melvill's description of this needlepoint strikes a faint bell on which note a modern account of Priscilla might end.

> The background material is very old and worn, and the embroidery is quite faded. The pattern is very nice and it would have been quite lovely when new.

16. Warm thanks to Jean F. Melvill for her February 15 and April 18, 1991, letters to the author.

3

Ancillary Ancestors: Bents and Middletons

with Richard E. Winslow III

> We are full of ghosts and spirits; we are as grave-yards full of
> buried dead . . . all our sires, verily, are in us. . . . We are
> fuller than a city.
>
> —*Mardi*, 1849

"Strange gaiety" has been detected in the early chapters of Melville's *Pierre*. Strange perhaps for Melville: he was euphoric. He had brought his "Whale" to a climax like nothing ever seen on these shores and created for America a full-blown tragic hero. The gifts and energy that unleashed his powers now welcomed the prospect of "summer afternoons in the country," the "green and golden world" of the oceanless Berkshires. But halfway through the new book, he read, in New York, hostile and uncomprehending reviews of *Moby-Dick*—also failed to get the advance on *Pierre* he expected and needed. His worst assessment of "the reading public" was proving true. If he wrote the Gospels in his century he'd die in the gutter. Now he would not have the recognition his genius had earned, or a simple living from writing. He was never the same as man or writer. But early in *Pierre* his spirits were very high.

Pierre the young hero is substantially autobiographical—except that he yearns above all things for a sister where Melville had four of them. Before he gets his wish he rejoices in his forebears, transparently Herman's. Like Pierre, Melville was of "double revolutionary descent. On both sides he sprung from heroes." As for roots, in his elevated mood he would tell Sophia Hawthorne that he was "of Scotch descent—of noble lineage—of the Lords of Melville & Leven. . . . We shall have him for a neighbor," she wrote happily.[1]

No doubt Herman had got his Scottish genealogy from his credulous father, but in fact modern research has improved on it. He belonged to "a junior branch of the distinguished Melvilles of Fife, stemming from one of William the Conqueror's Norman knights, Guillaume de Maleville."[2] Musing on family histories, Pierre observes that a large number of peerages were new—created by George III. Few living peers, he thought, could trace themselves to the "thief-knights of the Norman." But Melville was anything but a snob. The reverse: radically democratic. Now out of strong conviction he makes, for ordinary Americans of his age, a bold claim: "Hundreds of unobtrusive families in New England . . . might easily trace their uninterrupted lineage to a time before Charles the Blade"—that is, before 1660.

All the time Pierre is thinking this way, the author knows what his protagonist will soon discover, that he has an illegitimate half-sister out of whom the novel will grow. His uncle Thomas Melvill had encountered her as an adult in Boston shortly after the death of her father and Herman's. Neither Thomas nor Chief Justice Lemuel Shaw, present at the same encounter, doubted her identity for a moment. So far as is known (not very far), her half-brother never met her. But without her it is most unlikely that *Pierre* would ever have been written.

The matter at hand, however, is not the novel. It is instead a hunch that rests on Melville's: that when he considered obscure New England families whose lines might be traced back two centuries, it would have been natural to think of the forebears of his own obscure sister—those of her mother's family, that is, since he knew his father's were not "unobtrusive." In his opening mood he was gener-

1. Eleanor Melville Metcalf, *Herman Melville: Cycle and Epicycle* (Cambridge: Harvard University Press, 1953), 184.
2. Merton M. Sealts, Jr., "The Melville Heritage," *Harvard Library Bulletin* 34 (Fall 1986): 337.

ous of spirit. He would have liked to think that the ancestors of the unknown mother of this sister had a history, recoverable roots. Uncle Thomas learned her name: Ann Middleton Allen by her mother's hasty marriage. The older relative who accompanied her was named Bent. Bents and Middletons, English lineage as specified. They were living in Boston, where Allan, Herman's father, was born and raised. New Englanders, as specified.

Here, then, is an attempt to test Melville's breezy assertion by seeking out the antecedents of these people. It will not be done "easily." Indeed, without a head start, a book called *The Bent Family in America*[3] (which never mentions Ann Middleton Allen), such a search could hardly be attempted by untrained genealogists. Nor begun, for that matter, without hope that the tedium of sire to son, no less dame to daughter, may be relieved by the sort of curious facts and events that keep the fortunes of unknown people from being uninteresting.

I

1564 is a year to remember. Shakespeare was baptized at Stratford on April 26. Two months before that Christopher Marlowe was baptized at Canterbury. Eleven days earlier Galileo was christened in Pisa. In Rome three days later Michelangelo died. Early in the fall, in Penton-Grafton, county of Hampshire, the first entry was made in the Weyhill Parish record: *"Ede Bent filia Joannis bēt baptize est xvj Septembris 1564."* Joannis, first known of many John Bents, father of Edith, died in 1588 leaving the church twelve pence, the poor box six shillings and eight pence. His estate was inventoried at £13.0.6, a sum that would not buy a single passage to America, which would cost his daughter-in-law £17 (Bent, 10).

Robert Bent, brother of *Ede*, married Agnes Gosling in 1589. In 1596 they had a son, John, who about 1624 married a Martha ————, first in a line of Martha Bents that would reach to the mother

3. Allen H. Bent, *The Bent Family in America* (Boston: David Clapp & Son, 1900).

of Ann Middleton Allen. Probably because of a new tax on seacoast shires, John with his wife and four children in 1638 boarded the *Confidence*, "Intended for New-England." Some sixteen miles west of the little town of Boston the family settled in Sudbury, which was incorporated with fifty-four inhabitants on their arrival. Freeman and member of a Puritan church, John Bent (with Peter Bent, John How, and others) petitioned to "make a Plantation" near the Sudbury River.[4] How, first white settler of Marlborough, opened there a Black Horse Tavern in 1661 (*Hostelry*, 35). Then he deeded to David, his son by Martha, land in the new part of Sudbury where David built another tavern. In 1853 Henry Thoreau left his horse there over-night, and wrote: "How Tavern. The oldest date on the sign is 1716" (ibid., 48). In time it became known as the Red Horse Tavern and then, after the name Longfellow's book of verse gave it, the Wayside Inn. (*Tales of a Wayside Inn* celebrated "175 years" in the "family of Howes.")[5]

John, progenitor of American Bents, farmed his land, was active in local affairs, and fathered two more children here, Joseph (1641) and another Martha. Joseph's troubles would bring him to modern atten-tion, but his brother Peter Bent had them too. He built a gristmill in Marlborough which Indians burned, having already scalped his son, who survived. Then they burned down Marlborough. Two years later Peter died. His widow petitioned for support of seven children.

To advance this line rapidly for a moment, Peter Bent had a son Peter, who had a son Peter who lived to be ninety-one. His widow Mary died at ninety-three, and her daughter Mary, it is said, lived to be ninety-four (Bent, 22–23). This Mary Bent wed Joseph Fay; their daughter Elizabeth married Uriah Brigham and had a son Peter Bent Brigham, best known of American Bents. Born in 1807 near St. Albans, Vermont, he got a start opening and selling oysters in

4. C. F. Garfield and A. R. Ridley, *As Ancient Is This Hostelry: The Story of the Wayside Inn* (Sudbury, Mass.: Porcupine, 1988), 9.

5. As early Bents were involved in the famous How enterprise, so succeeding generations of Bents had a penchant for running taverns or inns. Elijah Bent, great-grandson of the first John, had an inn in what is now Wayland called the Pequot House, built about 1770 and in business over a century later. About 1775, "the Street Tavern" was kept by Nathan and Rufus Bent of Sudbury. And Lemuel Bent of Milton kept an eighteenth-century tavern on the Canton, Massachusetts, turnpike, which his widow continued (Bent, 44).

Boston. Next he became a restaurateur in the How-Bent tradition, running a large establishment in Boston's famous Concert Hall, which he would own. Through shrewd investments in real estate and railroads he built a huge fortune. A lifelong bachelor, Brigham on his death in 1877 willed his estate to the indigent sick. The result was a hospital called the Peter Bent Brigham, which in 1910 became Harvard Medical School as well—Brigham and Women's today.

It was not until 1986 that the spotlight fell on Joseph, first American-born Bent, son of the original John and Martha. He had made what looked like an advantageous marriage (Bent, 16). The bride was Elizabeth Bourne of Marshfield, whose father's sister had married the son of William Bradford, thirty-one times Governor of Plymouth Colony. Another aunt married Josiah Winslow, brother of Edward, who arrived on the *Mayflower*, was three times governor of Plymouth, and is remembered for his *Good News from New England* (1624). But the union was ill-starred. If Allen Bent's date for the wedding were correct, a son Joseph should have arrived over a year later. But when he did, his parents had been married three and a half months.[6]

For a monograph unhappily called *Sex in Middlesex*, Roger Thompson scoured the records of the Middlesex County Quarterly Courts (Middlesex is west and south of Boston). Even in the context of improper events, the marriage of Joseph and Elizabeth Bent was exceptional, as well as mysterious. With unmarried women in labor—or with those not married "long enough"—Massachusetts law followed English practice. Midwives were required to question women in childbirth as to the identity of the father. Spoken under such circumstances, the mother's word was considered incontrovertible. But when Mrs. Bent was brought to bed "she lied blatantly," writes Thompson, "as we shall see" (Thompson, 23). What is seen is that she was questioned about a week late, after "the navell string dyed off" (ibid.). Previously Joseph had "owned the child to be his, but now he claimed he had no knowledge of his wife" before they married. Under investigation, Mrs. Bent admitted that the father was James Taylor, with whom she had

6. Roger Thompson, *Sex in Middlesex: Popular Mores in a Massachusetts Colony, 1649–1699* (Amherst: University of Massachusetts Press, 1986), 23, 30, 58–59, 68–69, 173.

> had to doe severall times: & . . . Taylor said to her that *she*
> *should be silent* & he would begett a boy for Joseph who had
> spoken [proposed] to her once . . . & Joseph would not mind
> [know about] it & that James Taylor told her that he would
> speak to Joseph to come & he would tell him that she would
> have him. (Thompson, 58–59)

Joseph assured his parents that he was innocent, but there were
doubters. The baby, another Joseph, was about three months old
when Bent made a candid confession in church. First he acknowledged that through Satan and his "owne lust" he had fallen into the
sin of "uncleanes before marriage with Elizabeth." He further confessed that he was "well pleased that it was layd unto another, and
he sometyme of such family whose honor and good name. . . ."
Elizabeth successfully denied having had to doe with Taylor *while
espoused* to Bent, a "hanging matter." But the hand of a Puritan God
was heavy; the baby did not live past infancy. The parents moved to
Sudbury and had more children, including another Joseph. But in
1675—"by chance medley or causalty [casualty?]"—the father was
killed with a pistol held by his brother (Bent, 21). His widow returned
to Marshfield and soon died as well, leaving five children to her
parents.

When the grandparents died, the second Joseph Junior was placed
with an uncle, John Man of Milton, "who had married his mother's
sister" (Bent, 21), which looks like incest but may be pronoun
confusion. In any case, some Sudbury Bents moved a little southwest
to become Milton Bents, and some of these found their circumstances improved. John Man taught Joseph to read and write and put
him out to trade; he became a blacksmith. Milton was originally part
of Dorchester. It was also close to Dedham, home of Rachel Fuller,
whom Joseph married. (Of the Dedham Fullers, Rachel was a likely
forebear of Margaret Fuller, whose mother was of Canton, nearby.)
Joseph and Rachel had a son Joseph in 1701 who became a selectman,
a captain at Crown Point, and a resident of Milton's Brush Hill Road,
soon to be a prestigious address. This Joseph married Martha
Houghton—whereby another Martha Bent. Joseph and Martha were

the parents of Rufus Bent, grandfather of Ann Middleton Allen, Melville's half-sister.

To most it is a silly business, counting fingers to reckon the marital status of mothers at the time of conception. But it is serious business to some. Pregnant brides have been "widely investigated by demographers" and have "fascinated social historians," according to Roger Thompson, one of them (Thompson, 54). He also reports as a sort of rule-of-thumb quota that one of five brides in "early modern England" was pregnant. About the same ratio prevailed in early Maryland. The whole matter perplexes him: "Why could they not wait the few more weeks until marriage?" (which assumes they had heretofore been waiting). He generously speculates on several reasons, never taking into account the one Joseph Bent had blamed—lust.

Probably because they could not be found, dates of marriages and births are not always given in *The Bent Family*. But even with missing data, social historians should be gratified to learn that generations of Bents handily beat the odds of one in five, providing considerable precedent for Martha Bent's susceptibility to the boy Allan Melvill. Peter Bent, grandson of the original John, married a cousin thirty years his junior and gained a daughter in a month (Bent, 18). Peter Bent of Sudbury, great-grandson of John, wed Mary Parris, a minister's daughter, who was delivered of another Mary after two months and ten days. But this indiscretion may have been obscured by other distractions in the family.

By the time the baby arrived, Mary Bent's clerical father had died, having experienced more torment than Mary alone could inflict. It was Salem, 1692. "When these calamities first began," her father would write, "[it] was in my own family." Several weeks passed before "such hellish operations as witchcraft were suspected."[7] Through confession, repentance, and prayer, he managed to release his daughter (probably Elizabeth, Mary's older sister) from "sore fits of Satan" (Hansen, 24). Parris was thought to have sparked the whole tragedy by bringing home from Barbados the slave-woman Tituba, a Carib Indian who confessed to practicing witchcraft, intro-

7. Chadwick Hansen, *Witchcraft in Salem* (New York: George Braziller, 1969), 30.

ducing "occult experiments" with which the trouble apparently began. The hapless minister left Salem by popular demand, lived in
various places, and died in Sudbury (Bent, 24).

Mary Parris was far from the last pregnant Bent bride. Joel Bent
of Sudbury, great-grandson of John, fathered a daughter born six
months early (Bent, 34). Where records exist, the winner is yet
another Joseph Bent, another Milton blacksmith. His wife Mehitable
had a daughter one day short of a month into married life (ibid., 45).
His younger brother Rufus was not only the father of Martha Bent,
whom Allan inseminated at fifteen, but also of the esteemed Ann
Bent, widely known proprietress of a Boston ladies' goods store,
herself born a bit soon. (Herman's Uncle Thomas also encountered
her when he met Ann Middleton Allen.)

Among those about him, Rufus Bent was not a success. Identified
as a housewright, there is no record of his building any houses. His
father, Joseph of Milton, had two other sons who became army
captains like himself. By the time Joseph enlisted to serve in the
American Revolution at Boston, the British were long and permanently gone. He saw no action elsewhere. According to her lengthy
and most respectful obituary in the *Boston Evening Transcript* (March
13, 1857), Ann, his shopkeeping daughter, went to work very young
because of poverty in the family and "the absence of her father." It
is not always clear where he lived, or was absent from. He was
fruitful and multiplied, replenished some earth without subduing any,
and ended so quietly the family genealogist could not find him.

But Rufus Bent had made what looked like a fortunate marriage.
The bride was Ann Middleton McKenzie of Dorchester, a young
widow, daughter of Alexander Middleton, a Boston merchant who
arrived from Scotland about 1735. In 1771 or 1773 Rufus moved
from Milton to Boston, by which time he had three children by Ann:
two girls who remained single, and a son who died at sea. There
would be three more children, Ann, Martha and Prudence, birth-
places unknown. Ann Bent was to become the successful Boston
shopkeeper. Martha married Bethuel Allen, a farmer, in Canton, a
small town near Boston, before giving birth to Allan Melvill's daughter in 1798. Prudence married Silas Kinsley, who prospered in
prerailroad transportation. (Their son Rufus Bent Kinsley founded
the Kinsley Iron and Machine Company at Canton, which furnished

muskets to the government in 1812.[8]) Sarah married a Boston merchant named Barnard; their son Charles became a "rare philanthropist" (Bent, 46). The infusion of Middleton blood appears to have considerably improved the status of Bents.

It is surprising that Rufus Bent can be found in the excitement of Boston just before the Revolution. First this is because careful "Minutes of the Tea Meetings" were kept.[9] When it was resolved that the shipment from the East India Company would be returned and no duty paid, a watch was posted over cargo and vessel. Rufus Bent was a watchman. (There were two Rufus Bents on the scene; Rufus of Sudbury was a sailor in the war.) Almost two years after the ignominious British evacuation of Boston in March of 1776, Rufus enlisted in the army. His service record survives:

> Conductor, (late) Deputy Quartermaster General's department; enlisted Feb 18, 1779; discharged Sept. 23, 1780; service, 31 mos., at Boston; *also*, Wagon Master; list of men stationed at Boston [year not given].[10]

Glimpses of the veteran appear first in a document drawn up in his own clear hand. It had been ordered by the Common Wealth that inhabitants of certain Wards in the Town of Boston bring to a shop on Barrett Wharf "all weights and Measures made use of by them that the same be adjusted by a proper standard and sealed according to law." This notice was signed and dated May 30, 1781. Rufus responded with

Boston Feb. 11th 1782

By virtue of the within Precept I have warn'd the Several Wards of the Town of Boston N° 11 and N° 12

Rufus Bent A
Constobol of Boston

(signed)[11]

---

8. Kinsley's Company flourished hard by Paul Revere's Copper Works in Canton, Massachusetts; Revere's home was long a Canton showplace, along with the Old Stone Viaduct built by George Washington Whistler, Whistler's Father. See Mary S. Stimpson, "Canton Among the Blue Hills," *New England Magazine* 24 (March 1906): 120, 126.

9. *Proceedings of the Massachusetts Historical Society* 20 (1882–83): 10–15.

10. *Massachusetts Soldiers and Sailors of the Revolutionary War* (Boston, 1891), 1:977.

11. Samuel Phillips Savage Papers, Box 5, Massachusetts Historical Society, Boston.

On March 9, 1784, at Faneuil Hall he was sworn as constable again. Four years later he was paid £4 16s. for work on the South Meeting House. With that, but for *The Bent Family*, he might have disappeared.

The genealogist reports, however, that in 1798 Rufus was "living in Mariette, O." (46). This was a sort of New England town suddenly transplanted to a wilderness in 1788 largely through the efforts of General Rufus Putnam, now of the Ohio Company, which was granting lands to veterans who had been mustered out of the armed services, years before, with depreciated securities in lieu of pay. In July of 1793 the Company was still making allotments to "Settlers &c." Allotment N° 9 N.W. of Wolfcreek Mills was parcelled to ten men on July 15; on top of the list was Rufus Bent.[12] A census of 1800 has him in Marietta, also in 1803. He is on the Ohio Tax List in 1810 but was in fact no longer there. At some point he had made his way back to Massachusetts, thence to Canton, where he lived out his days with his presumably prosperous daughter Prudence Kinsley. (A plaque by a stream that powered Canton industries today remembers KINSLEY IRON WORKS.) Paul Revere was living in Canton; perhaps he and Rufus recalled each other from Boston days.

Allen Bent leaves Rufus in Ohio in 1798, having apparently not searched many graveyards. But not long ago on a dark day with a Scotch mist a private investigator examined stones in a somewhat obscure section of the Old Canton Cemetery at Canton Corner, "just north of a steepled wooden church." A gray slate stone in fair condition is among Kinsley graves. With a weeping-willow decoration at the top, the face reads:

In Memory of
Mr. Rufus Bent
who died
March 21 . . 1808
Aged 66 years.

12. A. B. Hulbert, ed., *Records of the Original Proceedings of the Ohio Company* (Marietta, 1917), 2:146.

Ann Bent has a larger, more ornate stone nearby, which on the back reads "Aunt Nancy"—what, according to a niece, the children called her. There is no sign of Mrs. Rufus Bent.

Nor knowledge of when the couple parted. Perhaps they separated for good when he went west, perhaps before that. He was a Patriot of sorts, and she, daughter of a Scottish merchant, may have felt otherwise. She had first married in Dorchester, and she ended there with her daughter Sarah McKenzie Barnard, also prosperous. Bent and Milton records agree; she died on July 31, 1807, also sixty-six, near where she had lived with her first husband.

By the time she died, her granddaughter Ann Middleton Allen, Melville's half-sister, was nine years old. Her daughter, Martha Bent Allen, had eight children by Bethuel, her husband. One was another Martha. This Martha Allen at twenty-two became engaged to William Gordon Means of Amherst, New Hampshire—where as a boy he had been educated—as were Allan Melvill and his good friend, the eventually famous Justice Lemuel Shaw, who like Thomas Melvill would later come in contact with Allan's illegitimate daughter in Boston. Martha Allen and William G. Means were married in the parlor of Ann Bent and Ann Middleton Allen next to their ladies'-goods store in Boston on Washington Street. In 1843 a daughter was born to this couple and named Anne Middleton Means. William became a colonel and a successful Boston businessman. Anne his daughter lived until 1923 and published a genealogy of her father's family.[13] Three years after her death a short account of her own life appeared.[14] She had become a reasonably affluent, unmarried, proper Bostonian, and marked the end of her line of Bent/Allens.

When Ann Middleton Allen was ten, back in 1853, that line touched again briefly the family of Melville, this time Herman. The year 1853 climaxed the efforts of the author's wife, mother, in-laws, and others to break the unremitting strain under which he labored at his desk. Everyone was worried about him, and those closest concentrated on an attempt to get him a consulship such as Hawthorne had been awarded by his friend Franklin Pierce. Melville was recommended to

13. Anne M. Means, *Amherst and Our Family Tree* (Boston: Privately printed, 1921).
14. In *The New England Historical and Genealogical Register* 80 (1926): 444–45.

the same President; among those pressing for the appointment was Justice Shaw. From Boston on May 3, Shaw wrote Caleb Cushing, political advisor to Pierce.

> I learn that my son-in-law . . . is a candidate for the consulship at Honolulu. . . . The family are well known to Mr. Sec. Marcy [William L., Secretary of State], and I rather think the Boston family are well known to the President, through their intimacy with that of Col Means of Amherst N. H.[15]

As remarked, Shaw had known about his friend Allan's by-blow since 1832, when he and Thomas had met Ann Middleton Allen in Boston. When he wrote of family intimacy between Boston Melvills and that of the Amherst Means did a special aspect of that intimacy cross his mind? In her genealogy, Anne Middleton Means would refer to her Allen namesake as "my mother's sister" (she may not have known it was half-sister) "for whom I was named" (Means, 316). Did Lemuel Shaw remember that this woman was half-sister to his son-in-law?

II

The widow McKenzie, first Ann Middleton, finally Mrs. Rufus Bent, was born in this country in 1741 and baptized at Trinity Church, Boston, on May 18. It was a tradition in her family that a Middleton ancestor had been at the head of King's College, Aberdeen, and from the frequency with which the name was bestowed on descendants it looks as if the Middletons were proud of it. The immigrant ancestor was Alexander Middleton, Jr. (baptized in 1709), a merchant who came from Scotland to Boston about 1735. The place was still but a town, and it is strange that his name appears so seldom in its affairs. It is on record that in Boston on November 10, 1735, he and Ann Todd, also from Scotland, announced their intention to

---

15. Jay Leyda, *The Melville Log* (New York: Harcourt, Brace & Co., 1951), 1:468–71.

marry, and in 1741 a daughter Ann was baptized. (They would have four more daughters.)

On December 7, 1747, Alexander and some sixty other citizens of standing signed a petition to license a Tavern or Inn on King Street to be called the Exchange (often the Royal Exchange) Tavern: "there seems to be a Necessity for it." (It became one of Boston's foremost; Middleton signed with a paraph broad as a sword.) He subscribed "for two" to a publication called *Prince's Chronology*, which claimed its readers were "justly regarded as the principal Literati of New England." He qualified for a two-page entry in a series called "Brief Memoirs and Notices of Prince's Subscribers," his sketch compiled by Emma Ware of Milton.[16] But it says nothing of his life here except that he married, and died in August 1750 (three years before his mother). What had engaged him, however, is revealed in the *Boston Gazette* for June 4/11, 1739, and despite fading can be made out almost in toto:

> To be sold by Alexander Middleton at Warehouse Number 3, in Butler's Row, Crown Glass in Cases uncut, Ditto in Chests cut in Squares, ordinary ditto cut in squares per the Chest, Bar and Sheet Lead, white and brown Earthen ware, Glass Bottles, Quarts & Pints, bottled Ale in Hampers, Grindstones, Flagstones, Cordage, C[——?], Nails, Corks, Pipes, glaz'd and ordinary ditto. And best Sunderland Coal on Board the ship Betty, William Foster, Commander, lying at the North side of the Long Wharff.

It was a good address. Butler's Row, at the foot of King Street leading directly onto Long Wharf, was occupied by "merchants of high standing." Very shortly after Alexander's death, the *Gazette* carried a related notice:

> To be sold by Ann Middleton, at the three Sugar Loaves, at the Lower End of King Street, Choice English Pickled Wallnutts, by the Hundred or Smaller quantity.

16. The memoir "Alexander Middleton" appeared in the *New England Historical and Genealogical Register* 52 (1898): 13–14. Its author, Emma Ware, was almost certainly a relative.

"Sugar" in the shop's name may hint at what was about to happen. On September 28, 1752, the widow Middleton and one David Fick announced the intention to wed, and on October 15 they did so at Trinity Church. Fick was but a foreman of a sugar refinery belonging to James Smith in Brattle Street. In marrying him, Mrs. Middleton appears to have lost legal control of her children. [17]

Ann Middleton McKenzie, daughter of Alexander and Ann Middleton, who married Rufus Bent of Milton, had a sister Prudence; she married Joseph Whipple, a surgeon in Paul Revere's regiment. Mary, the oldest sister, married James Lovell, son of the renowned "Master Lovell" (John) of Boston Latin, at Trinity Church. The story branches out in new relationships.

Master Lovell was a Tory and his son James a rebel spy, exposed when a letter of his was found on the body of General Joseph Warren after the Battle of Bunker Hill. Shipped in irons to Halifax, jailed (it is said) with Ethan Allen, exchanged for a general, James was sent to Congress. His wife, Mary Middleton Lovell, had a daughter Mary who wed Mark Pickard, an Englishman who had stocked Ann Bent's shop on Washington Street when it opened. (She sold imported goods on commission with long-lasting success.) Ann Bent and her sister Martha, mother of Ann Middleton Allen, were granddaughters of Alexander Middleton.

Mary and Mark Pickard had a child named Mary Lovell Pickard, who as a young woman lived in 1826 with her relatives Ann Bent and Ann Middleton Allen in their quarters on Washington Street. It was there in the parlor on June 11, 1827, that Mary Lovell Pickard married the Reverend Henry Ware, Jr., well-known Unitarian minister (Emerson's predecessor at the Second Church in Boston), writer, and Harvard professor. (Grandson of a Unitarian minister of Boston, T. S. Eliot would apparently have been named Henry Ware Eliot, Jr., but for an older brother who was given the name.) Mary Lovell Ware

17. Tradition has it, and Emma Ware's memoir of Alexander agrees, that as a matter of status Smith took a dark view of the alliance. He had married one of Ann Middleton's sisters and lived grandly in Milton. He and his wife, aunt to the Middleton girls, adopted and raised them on Brush Hill Road in a great mansion. Smith died there at eighty-one, and his widow, a second wife, conveyed the estate to her brother, a Loyalist. Unmarried daughters, Loyalists too, by report, lived out the Revolution in the mansion unharmed.

was made famous by an inspirational book, Edward B. Hall's *Memoir of Mary L. Ware* (Boston: Crosby, Nichols & Co., 1853). She wrote many letters from Brush Hill and spent her widowed years there. The marriage of Rufus and Ann Middleton Bent was only one of the many ties between two dissimilar families.

III

The Scottish ancestry of the Boston/Milton Middletons was as prominent as the English Bents' was obscure. But Alexander Middleton, Sr., is best remembered for an odd reason. Grandfather of Mrs. Rufus Bent, he was Controller of Customs at Aberdeen. But he eventually became known to history because of a boy who tended sheep in his fields. The shepherd boy was James Ferguson (1710–76), who was early and for twenty-six years remained a successful portrait painter, his means of support while achieving wide fame as a self-taught astronomer. Born to a laborer on Middleton's land, he learned to read while watching a brother being catechized. At seven he had three months of schooling; at eight he began tending sheep. Acquiring thread and beads to measure by, he mapped the stars. After he left Middleton's employ, an extraordinary butler became his mentor. Eventually he contrived rotulas and orreries "for showing the places of sun and moon for each day of the year, the times of eclipses, motions of the planets, etc." (A planetary machine he constructed survives.) In 1756 he had a huge success with a book, *Astronomy Explained on Sir Isaac Newton's Principles*, having devised a way of explaining complex phenomena in easy language. George III pensioned him and received him to discuss mechanics. But according to Ferguson's standard biography,[18] his domestic life was most

18. Ebenezer Henderson, *Life of James Ferguson, F.R.S.* (Edinburgh: A. Fullerton & Co., 1867). Henderson's wild and moralistic tale of Agnes's fate (279–85), composed over a century after she disappeared, has been foolishly accepted. The author claims he found a book called *The Female Jockey Club* which belonged to the very physician who attended Agnes Ferguson in her last hours. According to Blake, the doctor, "on January 27th, 1792, she ended her sad career in a garret, amid squalid poverty . . . near Charing Cross" (282). According to Henderson, Blake wrote a "short account" of her long misadventures on the flyleaf of this volume. She had run off with a nobleman who abandoned her; went to Fleet Street for debt;

unhappy. Its nadir came in 1763 when his beautiful and gifted daughter Agnes, walking on the Strand with her father, disappeared. She was eighteen, and he never saw her again. It is peculiar how his story relates to Bents and Middletons of Boston and their marriages.

In his 1876 biography of Ferguson, Ebenezer Henderson prints an "Extended Memoir" written by James Ferguson himself. But the "heaven-taught philosopher" neglected to name the man for whom he tended sheep while deciphering the solar system. Henderson makes a good deal of this before dramatically revealing that "his name was ALEXANDER MIDDLETON" (Henderson, 11). Then he proudly explains where he made this discovery: in "an American publication:—'A Memoir of Mary L. W. Pichard [sic],' Boston, U. S., 1856." Three strikes. (A redundant fourth would be a newspaper claim that the memoir was "probably by Dickens.") The woman's name, to repeat it, was Mary Lovell Pickard Ware. Her memoir, repeat, was written by Edward B. Hall, and the year was 1853. In his first chapter Hall describes Mary's childhood trip to Great Britain with her parents, their visits to relatives, and particularly to Alexander Middleton, her mother's relation: he was "a Scotch farmer in whose family Ferguson the astronomer lived as a shepherd-boy," Mary's exact words as printed by Hall, page 9. So Henderson discovered Middleton through Mary Ware, who had been living with Ann Bent and Ann Middleton Allen, themselves relatives.

Middletons, however, were distinguished in their own right. The claim of the family in America that an ancestor had been at the head of King's College, Aberdeen, turns out to be an understatement. The College (founded in 1493) had known two Middletons, father and son, as Principals. The father of Middleton the Controller and sheep owner was George Middleton, D.D., Dean of the Diocese of Aberdeen and Principal until 1717. His father, the Reverend Alexan-

---

led a life of "wildest dissipation" for almost thirty years, mostly right in London, etc., etc. The story, far too long to fit on a leaf of this small volume, reads exactly like one invented by the *author* of *The Female Jockey Club*, the anonymous Charles ("Louse") Pigott. Even more like *Memoirs of Mrs. Coghlan* (1794), the last part of which Piggot faked, the lady having died in midstream (see Philip Young, *Revolutionary Ladies* [New York: Alfred A. Knopf, 1977], 154, 159, 168–70, 210). Blake claims he wrote in January 1792 in a book that was not published until two years later. The *Dictionary of National Biography* soberly repeats the story of Agnes and the doctor.

der Middleton, had graduated from the college in 1630 and was made subprincipal in 1641. "Contrary to the foundation of the college" he took a wife, becoming the "first regent that entered into a marriage condition" (Ware, "Middleton," 13–14). Removed by Cromwell, he was promoted to Principal at the Restoration. "In his time the college flourished," according to Biscoe's *Earls of Middleton*, "as he caused good order to be kept therein" (Ware, 13). It might be noted that in 1575 a famous scholar, poet, and reformer of Scottish religion and universities, Andrew Melville, assisted Principal Arbuthnot of King's in forming a new university constitution (*Dictionary of National Biography* [*DNB*], 13:232).

The most famous Middleton was probably John (1619–74), a Major-General created First Earl of Middleton by Charles II and "prominent on both sides" in the civil war. (Cromwell once had him in the Tower for life, but he escaped in his wife's clothes and joined the exiled King in Paris.) He is often mentioned, as Emma Ware observed, "in the annals and histories of the period." Samuel Pepys first put him down in his diary (December 31, 1667) as a "dull, heavy man; but he is a great soldier."[19] Next year Pepys had a fresh perception: "a shrewd man, but a drinking man, I think" (Pepys, 9:325). Middleton was Commander-in-Chief in Scotland, 1660–63, and served out his days as Governor of Tangiers, where he died in 1674. Pepys's notion was apparently accurate; history says he died from a fall "met with in a fit of intoxication" (*DNB*, 13:354).

The father of John and Alexander, General and Principal, was Robert of Cauldham ("Caddam"), county of Kincardineshire. He is usually remembered for having been killed in his own house by men of Montrose invading Scotland in the name of the King. John the General partly avenged the deed by burning Montrose's castle, also in Kincardineshire. His oldest son was Charles (1640?–1719), Second Earl of Middleton and Secretary of State to James II. The most recent distinguished Middleton in this line was probably another Charles, who became First Lord of the Admiralty in 1804.

As for the remote past, history does not trace the Middletons

19. *The Diary of Samuel Pepys,* ed. Robert Latham and William Mathews (Berkeley and Los Angeles: University of California Press, 1974), 8:600–601.

farther back than Robert of Cauldham. But it does state that the family "owned the lands of Middleton, from which they took their surname, before the time of William the Lion" (*DNB*, 13:352). William the Lion, King of Scotland, was born in 1143 and crowned at Scone in 1165. Large of spirit, Herman Melville, or Melville as Pierre, might have liked those dates. Personally, and on behalf of little known New England families of their time.

TALES OF THE
BERKSHIRE BISHOPRIC

4

Intentional Grounding: The Lightning-Rod Man

It is a pity that Mr. Melville so often in conversation uses
irreverent language—he will not be popular here on that very
account—but this will not trouble him.
                          —Sarah Morewood to George Duyckinck,
                          December 28, 1851

He predicted it, but the reception of *Moby-Dick* was a disappointment
Melville never got over. He followed up in *Pierre* by killing off his last
major persona. Then with six books behind him he changed, turning
to shorter, different fictions. Six of these, all written at Pittsfield,
appeared in 1856 as *The Piazza Tales*. Three of them—"Bartleby,"
"Benito Cereno," and "The Lightning-Rod Man"—were first published in *Putnam's Monthly*. The first two of these tales are among
his best-known works; the third, shorter and less ambitious, is first
in a short special series of stories that have a "secret meaning."
These pieces have surface meaning, or apparent meaning, acceptable
to respectable magazines like *Putnam's*. But the author—and very
likely a choice few others—took primary pleasure in the "hidden"
Rabelaisian elements at the heart of things. Many, in an un-Victorian
age, are equipped to share this pleasure. But in the case of "The
Lightning-Rod Man" most readers, and apparently all Melville critics,
have not done so. The tale is said to have "excited great attention"
when first it appeared in 1854, and was reprinted in Burton's

Cyclopaedia of Wit and Humor (1858), thus becoming the only Melville short story available to the public for the rest of his life.[1] But the one reader who establishes that he understands is an American historian, British by birth and background.

"The Lightning-Rod Man" reads like a one act, one set, two-man play with sound effects. Blithely and prominently it has been labeled "what a single reading makes transparently clear: a straightforward light satire against the new breed of huckstering salvation sales-men."[2] Anyone who buys this misses the point entirely.

With "grand irregular thunder" and a man standing on the hearth-stone of his low cottage among the hills the scene opens. Scattered bolts boom overhead and crash down the valleys with "zig-zag irradiations, and swift slants of sharp rain" on the roof. "Hark!—some one at the door. Who is this that chooses a time of thunder for making calls? And why don't he, man-fashion, use the knocker?"

> "A fine thunder-storm, sir."
> "Fine?—Awful!"
> "You are wet. Stand here on the hearth before the fire."
> "Not for worlds!"
> . . . A lean gloomy figure. Hair dark and lank . . . sunken pitfalls of eyes . . . [which] played with an innocuous sort of lightning. . . . He stood in a puddle on the bare oak floor; his strange walking-stick vertically resting at his side.
> It was a polished copper rod, four feet long, lengthwise attached to a neat wooden staff, by insertion into two balls of greenish glass, ringed with copper bands. The metal rod terminated at the top tripodwise, in three keen tines. . . .
> "Sir," said I, bowing politely, "have I the honor of a visit from that illustrious god, Jupiter Tonans? . . . Ah, to the lover of the majestic, it is a good thing to have the Thunderer himself in one's cottage."

1. *The Piazza Tales and Other Prose Pieces, 1839–1860*, ed. Harrison Hayford, Hershel Parker, and G. Thomas Tanselle et al. (Evanston and Chicago: Northwestern University Press and The Newberry Library, 1987), 506, 599–600.

2. Warner Berthoff, ed., *Great Short Works of Herman Melville* (New York: Harper & Row, 1969), 187. It is possible that the story is most frequently encountered with this introduction in this paperback.

. . . the stranger eyed me, half in wonder and half in a strange sort of horror. . . .

"Good heavens!" he cried, starting—"there's another of those awful crashes. I warn you, sir, quit the hearth."

"Mr. Jupiter Tonans," said I . . . "I stand very well here."

"Are you so horridly ignorant, then, as not to know that by far the most dangerous part of a house during such a terrific tempest as this, is the fire-place?"

". . . Who are you?"

"I am a dealer in lightning-rods. . . . Hark, what Himmalayas of concussions! . . . In Criggan last month I put up three-and-twenty rods on only five buildings."

"Let me see. Was it not at Criggan last week . . . that the steeple . . . and the Assembly-room cupola were struck?"

". . . my workman was heedless." . . .

"Does your beat extend into the Canadas?"

"No. . . . Those Canadians are fools. . . . *Mine* is the only true rod. Look at it. Only one dollar a foot."

A contentious discussi... of lightning follows. The skies blacken—"it is dusk at noon." The "hooded mountains seemed closing and tumbling into the cottage."

"Will you order? Will you buy? Shall I put down your name?"

The host gets hotter.

"Who has empowered you, you Tetzel, to peddle your indulgences from divine ordinations? . . . I stand at ease in the hands of my God. . . . The scroll of the storm is rolled back. . . . Deity will not, of purpose, make war on man's earth."

"Impious wretch!" foamed the stranger, blackening in the face as the rainbow beamed.

The scowl grew blacker. . . . He sprang upon me, his triforked thing at my heart.

I seized it; I snapped it; I dashed it; I trod it; and dragging the dark lightning king out of my door, flung his elbowed, copper sceptre after him.

But spite of my treatment, and spite of my dissuasive talk to my neighbors, the Lightning-rod man still dwells in the land; still travels in storm-time, and drives a brave trade with the fears of man.

A telling, resonant little paragraph, that; a nice end to a tale that is not, plainly, transparent. What is to be made of the lightning rod? Why is the host so angry? Is the salesman really peddling salvation-protection, as alleged, from the hellfires of Calvinism?[3] Is there any connection between the narrator's refusal to buy and Ahab's defiance of lightning, so complete that in an awesome typhoon he will not allow the rods lying on his decks to be "grounded" in the ocean? (Is that because he is, as he admits, mad? Is, as has been suggested, the narrator here also a bit mad?) Or is Melville in the mood of Stubb, who says to Flask, "I suppose you would have every man in the world go about with a small lightning-rod running up the corner of his hat?" (*Moby-Dick*, Northwestern-Newberry Edition, 511.) One way around such questions has been to read "The Lightning-Rod Man" with a view to its author's recent experience.

What that had been, the late Jay Leyda explained forty years ago. Helen Morewood, Melville's great-niece, recalled that

her father told the story to her as an encounter that Melville had with a real lightning-rod salesman, who chose times of storms to pursue his trade. In the fall of 1853 the Berkshires were enduring an intense lightning-rod sales campaign, with advertisements and warnings and editorials on the subject in all the Berkshire papers. . . . Just at this time the Pittsfield Library Association listed among their new acquisitions, Cotton Mather's *Magnalia Christi Americana*, a troubling and frightening record of religion in its most bullying and bigoted aspect, and there was Melville's theme . . . in the Sixth Book,

3. This interpretation originates in the Hendricks House edition of *The Piazza Tales*, 1948.

Chapter III . . . "Relating Remarkables done by thunder." Among the Reverend Mather's listed admonitions is: IV. A fourth voice of the glorious God in the thunder, is *make your peace with* God *immediately, lest by the stroke of his thunder he take you away in his wrath.*[4]

In 1948, a year earlier, Egbert Oliver, editor of the Hendricks House edition of *The Piazza Tales*,[5] had taken a bigger step in identifying Jupiter Tonans himself as "probably" the Reverend John Todd, pastor of the Congregational First Church of Pittsfield from 1842 to 1873, and recognized throughout the Berkshires and western Massachusetts as "a kind of bishop."[6] "He never swerved," claimed Oliver, "from a firm belief in the Calvinism of Jonathan Edwards, a sufficient grounding in belief in divine wrath to familiarize him with heaven-hurled fire." As mentioned in Melville's story, a church Assembly-room (Todd's) was struck by lightning in 1835 (presenting a spectacular display during a "pretty full prayer meeting," vividly described in J.E.A. Smith's *History of Pittsfield, 1800–1876*,[7] a book to which Melville contributed an excellent sketch of his favorite uncle, Major Thomas Melvill, Jr.). Oliver also observed that the description ("caricature" might be better) of the rod man in the story is "entirely compatible with the pictures of the Reverend Todd" published in his two best known books. He did not notice that Jupiter Tonans bears Todd's initials.

Though his facts are askew, it is more than probable that Oliver spotted the target of Melville's satire in the tale—and by extension any who prey on the fears of men and women. Satirist and target, oddly, were two of Pittsfield's most noted citizens. *The Pittsfield Sun* for November 11, 1858, coupled their names as "gentlemen who are ready to lecture upon interesting subjects when applied to . . . The

4. *The Complete Stories of Herman Melville*, ed. Jay Leyda (New York: Random House, 1949), xxvi–xxvii. Leyda notes that Margaret Morewood recalled a copy of the book at Arrowhead, Melville's farm.

5. (New York, 1948), 238–41.

6. John Todd, *The Story of His Life Told Mainly by Himself*, compiled and partly written by his son John E[dwards] Todd (New York: Harper & Brothers, 1876), 494.

7. Two volumes (Boston: Lee and Shepherd, 1869, 1876), 2:239–40.

Rev. TODD of this town . . . is one of the best . . . Herman MELVILLE, Esq., of this town, the author, is also ready."

A "sparkling," good humored and popular speaker (as Melville was not), Todd never, however (writes his son), sparkled in the pulpit, and was far from fiery. (His "lightning," remarked Melville's narrator, was "innocuous.") "His preaching was always grave, and almost always solemn" (*Life*, 451). He lacked both the rigidity and the fire of the Calvinist spirit. "His own nature was one of deep tenderness," and he was "a little prone to melancholy." But his "enthusiasm" won over the "young and progressive, and kept the galleries of his church crowded with young men. . . . In ardor and hopefulness and sympathy with all that was bright and active and enthusiastic, he was abreast with any." Except for burning mountains in the distance, there were no fires in his vision of hell: "dreary, barren, parched fields," rather, and "rivers like ink," "dark openings that yawn like caverns"—"not a green spot . . . not a single flower, not a star in all the darkened heavens" (*Life*, 456). There is no Divine Wrath in his autobiography. He called Jonathan Edwards "a giant in theology," not the pulpit, and praised most "his meekness and gentleness under an ordeal that few could endure" (at Northampton, where Todd would later serve and name his church Edwards). He never preached, so he writes, against "any particular *amusements*—theatres, dramas, card-playing and the like . . . though I was never in a theatre, at the opera, or in a ballroom; never saw a game of cards or billiards played" (422). The lecture room at the Pittsfield church was once used by a traveling company to perform "The Reformed Drunkard"; he never again used the room himself. This is not much in the way of Calvinism.

But to think of Todd as a follower of Jonathan Edwards, and of Edwards as author of "Sinners in the Hands of an Angry God," might well result in thinking that Melville could, as Oliver has it, cast him in the role of lightning rod salesman out to terrify people. Yet neither in his pulpit nor in his ministry did he fit the part. Neither, of course, did Jonathan Edwards fit his. His famous sermon is highly atypical and, it is reported, was calmly delivered. He did supply "a vehicle which ignorance and crudity soon adopted," and thus "wrought incalculable harm." But "the main current of American revivalism flows from Whitfield and the Methodists."[8]

Assuming, as seems safe, that Melville did look into Mather's *Magnalia* on thunder and lightning, it is likely that he did have it in mind when he composed his own storm in the story. The Fire of God, explains Mather, "is *conceived to have been some* terrible Flash *of Lightning.*" In the Heavens: *"There Satan can . . . command much of the Magazine* of Heaven, *where that* dreadful Artillery . . . *Thunder and Lightning, are stor'd and lodg'd.*" God is "the high THUNDERER." "Lightnings" are "The *Arrows of God.* . . . The *Arm* that can wield *Thunder bolts,* is a very *mighty Arm*" (London, 1702).

But it appears that John Todd is satirically portrayed as the man with the lightning rod for entirely different reasons than Egbert Oliver gave. It was neither from the pulpit nor as pastor that he preyed on human fears. It was from the privacy of his study that issued one book that made him famous and did the damage. *The Student's Manual: Designed by Specific Directions to Aid in Forming and Strengthening the Intellectual and Moral Character and Habits of the Student* by Rev. John Todd, D.D.,[9] available practically everywhere books were sold or loaned, gave little or no thought to a student's salvation. Rather it advised young men to fix their religious principles early in life so as not to be distracted when they should be in single-minded pursuit of something else: "That upon which the young man fixes his eye . . . is SUCCESS." Hellfire, or any other afterlife, is quite out of the picture.

The guilt, fear, and dread—acute, persistent, irrational—to which Todd set fire were rather more immediate. A mere seven pages (145–52) nearly buried in the *Manual* were what brought "dusk at noon." They arrive in a chapter called "Reading" when the topic

8. Perry Miller, *Jonathan Edwards* (New York: William Sloane, 1949), 148. According to Miller, Edwards's most profound belief was in the unity of the race. "The investigator of depravity, the dissector of spiders, found in the depth of sin the basis for a new definition of the brotherhood of man that merged all men into one conception, that discomfited the prosperous and the proud, the merchants and the river gods, by telling them that in the nature of things God treats them all as one, along with Negroes and Hussantunnucks" (278–79).

9. Northampton: Hopkins, Bridgman & Co., 1835. In 1839, just short of his sixteenth birthday, Allan Melville, Herman's younger brother, acquired the book, which was already in its seventh edition. It came to rest in the Berkshire Atheneum with other Melville books. The copy at hand is the Twenty-Fourth edition, 1859.

turns to "Bad Books." These can be worse than "all the talents in hell, if the object were to pollute and to ruin . . . If you have an enemy . . . into whose heart you would place vipers which will live, and crawl, and torment him through life, and whose damnation you would seal up for the eternal world, put in his hand" such a book (Byron is fine) as will "pollute his imagination." This leads straight to physical pollution, "the frequent cause of sudden death. The apoplexy waits hard by . . . upon this sin. May not the pale-faced youth . . . tremble as he looks off the abyss . . . ?" Edwards's Sinners are Todd's Readers. He turns to Latin, here translated, to "say what I could not say in English." From ONANIS SCELUS (heinous) all minds greatly deteriorate; individuals become *imbecilem* (literally "without rod or staff"). The soul crumbles, God's punishment is certain.

It takes but a "single page" of Byron to chain upon the reader a "putrid carcass which [he] can never throw off." Todd is bold: has *he* ever read Byron? "And Moore, Hume [*David* Hume?], and Paine, Scott, Bulwer and Cooper?" "Yes, he has read them all, and with too much care." (His immunity is left mysterious.) Onanism is inevitable from the start. "The leprosy fills the whole soul"; "time only increases it." A paramount threat is mental derangement. "Physicians testify" that the vice is what fills the wards. Once *in* Insane Hospitals, Superintendents say, it is also "an almost insuperable obstacle" to the patient's recovery. At this point the author invites the reader to "a thrilling and harrowing chapter in [Benjamin] Rush on Diseases of the Mind" (1812).

The reverend doctor seems never to have suspected he had just blown the secret of his own sick success with the *Manual*. And supplied as well the reason for Melville's narrator's unfrightened anger at the rod salesman. It was readers of *Putnam's* who were supposed to take his piece of copper with the glass balls for what he was selling, and lightning the thing to be feared. To add menace, this "thing," as Melville calls it, terminates in three keen tines—a trident, which over centuries has carried various meanings, and is often pictured in the hand of the devil. It is a sign of him, his rod or sceptre, which Melville called the salesman's.[10] With the tines at his

10. It was illustrated as a pitchfork in a vignette for the tale's appearance in Burton's *Cyclopaedia*. This was the only original illustration for any signed Melville work printed in his lifetime. (Reproduced in *Piazza Tales*, 599.)

heart, Melville drags Todd out the door, and smashes to bits the symbol of one who still dwelled in the land, driving a brave trade with male fears. (Todd was not much concerned with females.)

If this Melville tale were a transparent, straightforward light satire, the anger felt by its narrator would be pointless and unaccountable. So also would be at least one vocal exchange between the combatants. When the salesman explains lightning—specifically the business about the downward stroke and then "the returning-stroke . . . when the earth, being overcharged with the fluid, flashes its surplus upward," and the narrator replies "The returning-stroke . . . Better and better"—what exactly (for the innocent) is "better"? When the salesman says Canadian lightning-rod makers are fools—"Some of them knob the rod at the top, which risks a deadly explosion"—what is the point if not bawdy?

When in anger the host calls the unwelcome guest a "Tetzel" (a different matter), what is the transparent meaning? ("Who has empowered you, you Tetzel, to peddle round your indulgences from divine ordination?") Johann Tetzel (J. T. again), c. 1465–1519, became a notorious "salesman"[11] of indulgences—for the dead, among others. Todd's church burned down soon after Melville moved to Pittsfield; there was a strenuous drive for pledges to rebuild it. ("Shall I put down your name?" demands the rod man.) Tetzel for some time sold his protection to promote the rebuilding of St. Peter's. He dwelt on the cheapness of his services. "Only a dollar a foot" (see Oliver, 241).

A failure of reading explains as well such critics as have questioned the "irrational" fearlessness of the host and his contempt for the hawker. Several have complained that the rod man has the better of the dispute: he is "the more reasonable" of the antagonists and represents, of all things, "the world of sanity and order."[12] The narrator has no use for the salesman because he sees, as the reader is meant to, the lightning rod for a fictional front and is in contempt of the ignorant author of a billion fears. The deepest dig at Todd was mention of the salesman's "sunken pitfalls of eyes," "ringed by indigo

---

11. *Encyclopaedia Britannica*, 15th ed., 11:661.

12. See, for example, William B. Dillingham, *Melville's Short Fiction, 1853–1856* (Athens: University of Georgia Press, 1977), 172–78.

halos": dark-circled sunken eyes (along with pallor) were supposed to be the surest sign of the Onanist.[13]

The British-American who in print has understood Todd and Melville in their fictional roles is G. J. Barker-Benfield of the Department of History, State University of New York, Albany. This fact *is* transparent in his *Horrors of the Half-Known Life: Male Attitudes toward Women and Sexuality in Nineteenth-Century America* (New York: Harper & Row, 1976). Part III of this book—eight chapters— is devoted to Todd, chiefly as he appears in his *Life* and the *Manual*. Barker-Benfield does not deal with the Melville story itself, but the title of his whole section on Todd says it all: "The Lightning-Rod Man." As his *Life* and the son who compiled it reveal, Todd was a man possessed. He was obsessed with tools, guns, fishing rods, canes (which last he named for their owners). For weeks in the woods by the streams he would tote enough tackle to furnish a small store; "but," writes the son, "he could hardly ever be persuaded to fish" (*Life*, 480). He bought every new gun or rifle as it appeared, and named each one as "a kind of pet. Not that he ever did much shooting." His sanctum, however, was his workshop; shelves crammed with bottles and tools—"several hundred tools"—with handles (as illustrated in the *Life*, 489). In the dark Todd could lay a hand on any one. But outranking all others was one "noble, sublime, curious, unappreciated instrument . . . the *lathe!*" he wrote. The only thing he prized more was a fountain featured in the center of his study—almost three feet high, appropriate in form (illustrated in *Life*, 430), and magical in enjoyment.

Of course Todd was scarcely first to clothe a common habit in terror. Francis Bacon as early as 1627 warned that "the cause of dimness of sight is the expense of spirit."[14] The first volume devoted

---

13. There is a funny burlesque of the practice in *Typee*, called "Producing a Light á la Typee." Kory-Kory starts a fire by rubbing his small stick against a big one, panting and gasping "as he approaches the climax," and a "delicate wreath of smoke curls spirally into the air" (*Typee*, Northwestern-Newberry Edition, 111–12). Kory-Kory's less innocent counterpart is Carlo with his hand-organ in *Redburn*. It sings to Carlo when he is sad, and cheers him. "Play on . . . Italian boy!" says Redburn, "while I list to the organs twain—one yours, one mine—let me gaze fathoms down into thy fathomless eye" (*Redburn*, Northwestern-Newberry Edition, 248–50). While in the Berkshires Melville wrote, beside "The Lightning-Rod Man," two other phallic-oriented tales, "Cock-a-Doodle Doo!" and "I and My Chimney."

14. Eric Partridge, *Shakespeare's Bawdy* (New York: E. P. Dutton, 1969), 187.

to the subject appeared in 1707; by mid-century the phobia was in
full force. There was spirited competition to see who could invent
the worst horrors. (Possible winner was a French entry of 1758, an
onaniste "who dried out his brain so prodigiously that it could be
heard rattling in his skull.") In the early decades of this century
endless pamphlets helped spread the word. Not until 1940 did
correction begin to see print: real harm resulted from guilt and
worry, as sold by Dr. Todd.

Melville was a "modern" in more ways than one. While he vented
his opinion of the bishop in a short fiction, that earnest gentleman
may be pictured with his precious fountain. It was glass-topped with
a basin beneath, in the center of which were "nearly forty little holes
in a circle, each hole just large enough to admit a very fine needle,"
he wrote.

> I have only to touch a little brass cock, and up leaps the water
> . . . nearly forty little streams . . . two feet into the air, and
> then turned into a myriad of silver drops, bright as diamonds,
> leaping and laughing as they rise and fall . . . I can think of
> nothing but pearls dropping into a well, or golden balls falling
> into cups of silver. With what profusion the jewels are tossed
> out! (*Life*, 429.)

Why don't he use the knocker?

5

Experimental Melville: "Cockeye-Doodle-Dee!"

Worst or nearest was a moronic bugler of a cock, playing
tenor to the neighbors' alto, with his room-rattling reveille.
"Cock-a-Doodle-do," Guy decided, was one of the world's
great euphemisms.
          —Martin Amis, *London Fields*

Feeling low on a spring morning, the narrator of "Cock-a-Doodle-
Doo!" walks his pasture in the first person. The air is damp,
disagreeable. Over a distant village rests "a great flat canopy of
haze, like a pall." He thinks of a terrible accident on the Ohio, in
which a friend was "sloped into eternity." And of a crash on the
nearby railroad where

> two infatuate trains ran pell-mell into each other, and climbed
> and clawed each other's back; and one locomotive was found
> fairly shelled, like a chick, inside of a passenger car in the
> antagonist train; and near a score of noble hearts, a bride and
> her groom, and an innocent little infant, were all disembarked
> into the grim hulk of Charon, who ferried them over, all
> baggageless, to some clinkered iron-foundry country or
> other.

"A miserable world!" And a "dunning fiend, my creditor, who frightens the life out of me. . . . I can't pay this horrid man."[1]

"Hark! By Jove, what's that? . . . What a triumphant thanksgiving of a cock-crow! 'Glory be to God in the highest!' . . . I begin to feel a little in sorts again. . . . And just now in the doleful dumps." It will be brown stout and a beefsteak for breakfast. "See the azure smoke of the village, like the azure tester over a bridal-bed" (C, 271–72). Back home, as he is reading *Tristram Shandy*—"a fine joke about my Uncle Toby and the Widow Widman"—the fiend calls. When he will not listen to the joke, narrator throws him out bodily. Now the whole country is "bathed in a rejoicing sunlight." The cock crows at noontide. "I felt as though I could meet death, and invite him to dinner . . . in pure overflow of self-reliance." The evening crow was "miraculous . . . victorious over the entire day" (C, 274–75).

> Where lurked this valiant Shanghai—this bird of cheerful Socrates—the game-fowl Greek who died unappalled?[2] . . . My princely, my imperial Shanghai! my bird of the Emperor of China! Brother of the Sun! . . . Tell me your master! (C, 275)

A "Great Bell of St. Paul's swung in a cock's throat" (C, 276). If at times "I would relapse into my doleful dumps, straightaway at the sound . . . my soul, too, would turn chanticleer, and clap her wings." He will find the noble cock, "clap the added mortgage on my estate," and buy him. But for a time he cannot find him, and others do not hear the wonderful sound. Finally one morning he sees outdoors a "certain, singular man" who has sawed and split wood for him, come for his pay. He had first noticed the fellow while reading Burton's *Anatomy of Melancholy*, brought him in, and fed him a good dinner.

---

1. Herman Melville, "Cock-a-Doodle-Doo!" *The Piazza Tales and Other Prose Pieces*, ed. Harrison Hayford, Hershel Parker, and G. Thomas Tanselle (Evanston and Chicago: Northwestern University Press and The Newberry Library, 1987), 269–70. Further citations will be noted parenthetically in the text as *C*.

2. Just before this Melville wrote, "oh, bird rightly offered up by the invincible Socrates, in testimony of his final victory over life"—a traditional, not historical, reading. After he drank the cup, according to Plato in the *Phaedo*, Socrates said only, "Crito, we owe a cock to Asklepios; pray do not forget to pay the debt." No one knows more.

The man has a "long saddish face, yet somehow a latently joyous eye. . . . His name was Merrymusk . . . how jolly a name for so unjolly a wight" (*C*, 280–81). He has a wife and four children, the woman "a perfect invalid," the youngsters all sick. He works hard and brings them food.

> "My friend," said I, "do you know of any gentleman here-abouts who owns an extraordinary cock?"
> "I know of no *gentleman*," he replied, "who has what might be called an extraordinary cock." (*C*, 281)

Paying what he could, the narrator promises to visit in a day or two with the remainder. And one fine morning he sallies forth into lonely country with "a mountain on one side (which I call October Mountain . . .), and a thicketed swamp on the other, the railroad cutting the swamp." Merrymusk's "wretched shanty" is hard to find, but the cockcrow becomes ever more distinct. Then at last he spies "the most resplendent creature that ever blessed the sight of man" (*C*, 281–82).

> Such a cock!
> "It is my cock!" said Merrymusk, looking slyly gleeful out of the corner of his long, solemn face. . . . It chipped the shell here. I raised it."
> "What will you take for Signor Beneventano?[3] . . . I will give you fifty dollars. . . . One hundred! . . . Five hundred!"
> "Bah!"
> "And you a poor man?"
> "No, don't I own that cock, and haven't I refused five hundred dollars for him?" said Merrymusk. . . . Trumpet! hither, boy, hither!" . . . The cock followed us into the shanty.
> "Crow!"
> The roof jarred.

3. The narrator explains what Melville himself had done: experienced this singer in an Italian opera, "claid in rich raiment, like to plumage . . . on the point of tumbling over backward with exceeding haughtiness." The tale is subtitled "Or, The Crowing of the Noble Cock Beneventano."

The visitor glances around the room. "Bare rafters overhead, but solid junks of jerked beef hanging from them," potatoes and cornmeal in corners. A blanket hangs at one end, behind which can be heard the ailing voice of a woman and her young.

"Merrymusk, will you present me to your wife and children?" In back of the curtain lay a "wasted, but strangely cheerful human face," the body too shrunken beneath the coverings to show. A pale girl sat beside her. In another bed, three children "side by side: three more pale faces." The guest asks if there is any hope of the wife's recovery?

> "Not the least."
> "The children?"
> "Very little."
> "It must be a doleful life. . . ."
> "Haven't I Trumpet? He's the cheerer. . . . Didn't *my* cock encourage *you*?" (*C*, 284–86)

Merrymusk is not seen again for some weeks. But hearing the rejoicing crow, narrator assumes that things are as usual. His own mind rejoices; he piles another mortgage on his estate and buys many bottles of porter and stout: "oh noble cock!" Then he thinks to call on his owner. Approaching the shack he feels odd misgivings, but is firmly bid to enter. The place is now a hospital. The man lies on a pile of clothes, the wife and children all in bed.

> "You are sick, Merrymusk," said I mournfully.
> "No, I am well," he feebly answered.—"Crow, Trumpet."
> "How is Mrs. Merrymusk?"
> "Well."
> "And the children?"
> "Well. All well."

This last is "shouted forth in a kind of wild ecstasy." His head fell back. "A white napkin seemed dropped upon his face. Merrymusk was dead." An awful fear grips the visitor. The cock crows.

"My good man is just dead," breathed the woman lowly. "Tell me true?"

"Dead," said I.

She falls back, dead in sympathy. "The cock seemed in a rapture of benevolent delight." He gives a final crow, as if he meant to "waft the wood-sawyer's soul sheer up to the seventh heavens." Then he does the same at the woman's bed. The pallor of the children is "changed to radiance. Their faces shone celestially." Trumpet seems bent on crowing their souls out of their wasted bodies. "I saw angels where they lay" (*C*, 288). Flown to the top of the house, the cock sounds "one supernatural note" and drops dead at narrator's feet. Now in the "hilly region . . . nigh the railroad track, just beneath October Mountain, on the other side of the swamp," stands a gravestone with a lusty crowing cock chiseled on it, and the words

—"Oh! death, where is thy sting?
Oh! grave, where is thy victory?"
(*C*, 288)

The narrator has buried family and cock and planted the stone. Yet has never since felt the doleful dumps, but he crows with a continual elongated crow:

COCK-A-DOODLE DOO!—oo!—oo!—oo!—oo!

Bold, shocking, final. But what is the point of the story? There is nothing like consensus, little agreement, general avoidance of the question. Has the tale teller lost his wits? Is his cockcrow sane? Ironic? Foolish? What killed the Merrymusks—and Trumpet? How is one supposed to respond? Newton Arvin, a great admirer of Melville, disliked the tale;[4] Henry Mills Alden, editor of *Harper's* for fifty years (he published Henry James), called it "about the best short story he ever read."[5] One approach would begin by rejecting the most wide-

4. Newton Arvin, *Herman Melville* (New York: Viking, 1950), 234–35.
5. Melville, "Cock-a-Doodle-Doo!" 510.

spread—not universal—theory about the piece,[6] which springs from Thoreau's essay "Walking," where he writes:

> The singer can easily move us to tears or laughter, but where is he who can excite in us a pure morning joy? When, in doleful dumps, breaking the awful stillness of our wooden sidewalk on a Sunday, or, perchance, a watcher in the house of mourning, I hear a cockerel crow far or near, I think to myself, "There is one of us well, at any rate,"—and with a sudden gush return to my senses.[7]

There it is, the very heart of it. Even "doleful dumps," the signature. Early depression taken for a walk, heartening cockcrow rushing good spirits back to the walker. It matters not to those who announce or support this discovery that Melville published his story in December 1853 in *Harper's Monthly*, having written it in the previous spring or summer. Thoreau's "Walking" first appeared posthumously in the *Atlantic Monthly* for June 1862 and reappeared in his book *Excursions*, 1863. The argument, moreover, is that the obvious source points to the tale's meaning: it satirizes Thoreau and Transcendentalism, their excessive egocentricity and antimaterialism. ("Overflow of self-reliance.") How Melville got his central idea and a key phrase from a Thoreau essay nine years in the future can be explained to their own satisfaction by those who think he did. He did not know Thoreau. But Hawthorne did, and Hawthorne knew Melville. Melville was in Concord sometime during the winter of 1852–53 and saw Hawthorne there. (On December 2, 1852: Hershel Parker's discovery.) Perhaps Hawthorne had seen some early version of "Walking" that Thoreau had composed as a lecture. Perhaps he was so impressed with the lines that he wrote them down, and maybe showed them to Melville, who might have copied them. (It is,

---

6. This implausible theory goes back forty years. See Egbert Samuel Oliver, " 'Cock-a-Doodle-Doo!' and Transcendental Hocus-Pocus," *New England Quarterly* 21 (1948): 207–9; William Bysshe Stein, "Melville Roasts Thoreau's Cock," *Modern Language Notes* 74 (1959): 5–10; Allan Moore Emery, "The Cocks of Melville's 'Cock-a-Doodle-Doo!' " *ESQ* 28 (Second Quarter) (1982): 89–111; and R. Bruce Bickley, Jr., *The Method of Melville's Short Fiction* (Durham: Duke University Press, 1975), 62.

7. Henry D. Thoreau, *Excursions* (Boston: Ticknor, 1863), 212.

after all, believed in some crannies that the chapter "Monday" from Thoreau's *Week*—which Melville *had* read—also lies behind the story, but the argument is unintelligible.)[8] In any event, the idea that the tale is satirical rings no known bell. In the name of Transcendentalism, who is being satirized? Not Merrymusk, who is treated tenderly and with respect. Narrator is, for the nonce, an obvious Melville persona, living in Pittsfield, Massachusetts, as did the writer at the time. The walk to the shanty, with the hills, the swamp, the railroad, and October Mountain is easily traced on the topographical map called Pittsfield East Quadrangle.[9] The author satirizes himself? How? Is Trumpet a goat, not a cock? According to Martin Green, the critics have willfully misunderstood. "It is surely wilful to interpret a story as being about Emersonian self-reliance when the principal character is called Merrymusk and his principal feature is that he 'possesses an extraordinary cock.' "[10]

The crowing of a cock or rooster has surely heartened many an early riser—depression lifted by music. Neither Thoreau nor Melville had to dream up "doleful dumps." In all these years no one seems to have seen it sitting in Bartlett's *Familiar Quotations* in the Anonymous section on the same page (917, 15th edition, 1980) as "O western wind, when wilt thou blow?" "Alas, my love! Ye do me wrong," and "Greensleeves was all my joy." Stanza One of "A song to the Lute in Musicke" goes:

> Where griping griefs the heart would wound
> And doleful dumps the mind oppress,
> There music with her silver sound
> With speed is wont to send redress.

Shakespeare gave these lines with minor changes to Peter, servant to Juliet's nurse, in Act IV, Scene v, of *Romeo and Juliet*. They had appeared in *The Paradyse of Daynty Devises*, collected by Richard Edwards in 1576, there called "In Commendation of Musick." Doleful

8. Oliver, " 'Cock-a-Doodle-Doo!' and Transcendental Hocus-Pocus," 207–9.

9. "Pittsfield East, Massachusetts" (Reston, Va.: U.S. Geological Survey, 1973).

10. Martin B. Green, *Re-Appraisals: Some Commonsense Readings in American Literature* (New York: Norton, 1966).

dumps are "thickly dispersed" in John Grange's "novel" *The Golden Aphrodite* (1577), which begins, "I haile ye Lidian streams: what meane these doleful dumps?" The verses were early set to music (four parts in D minor) from "an ancient manuscript"; the first stanza was supplied with new music, complex and dissonant, for Soprano and Piano in 1975.[11]

Melville's knowledge of *Romeo and Juliet* is obvious to any who have read the early chapters of *Pierre*. The notion that he was indebted to Thoreau, the object of his satire, persists at least to 1982.[12] What no one seems to have missed is his use of Wordsworth, where Melville awkwardly rewrites two familiar lines ("We poets in our youth begin in gladness / But thereof come in the end despondency and madness") like this:

> . . . Of fine mornings,
> We fine lusty cocks begin our crows in gladness;
> But when eve does come we don't crow quite so much,
> For then cometh despondency and madness. (*C*, 272)

("Cocks are generally good at dawn," comments Richard H. Fogle, "but they have little staying power. Will this rooster be able to keep it up?")[13] (Any number can play.)

Invoking "Resolution and Independence," Melville adds an overtone to his story. The Poet had made a sunrise excursion, sunk in dejection, and met a man "not all alive nor dead" but still with a flash in his eyes. As frequently remarked, the woodcutter calls up a leech-gatherer—both dreamlike figures who provide strength. (A few have thought of Trumpet as Merrymusk's Nightingale: "Now more than ever seems it rich to die, / . . . while thou art pouring forth thy soul abroad / In such ecstasy!")

It is established as well that, having mentioned *Tristram Shandy*,

11. The early version appears in Sir John Hawkins's *General History of the Science and Practice of Music* ([1776; rpt. New York: Dover, 1963], 2:924), with the words (mistakenly, it appears) attributed to Edwards himself. The modern treatment by Charles Wuorinen is published by C. F. Peters, New York.

12. Emery, "The Cocks of Melville's 'Cock-a-Doodle-Doo!' " 89–111.

13. Richard Harter Fogle, *Melville's Shorter Tales* (Norman: University of Oklahoma Press, 1960), 29.

Melville makes good use of it. The fine joke about Uncle Toby and the Widow Wadman, spoken of early in the story, is well known, and introduces the organ Melville will center on. Merrymusk's shanty is the backside of Shandy-Hall, where from his birth the matter of Tristram's *nose* is a distinguished precedent for Merrymusk's cock. The more Tristram insists that by *Nose* "I mean a Nose, and nothing more or less," the less convincing it becomes; finally he has to depend on the "cleanliness" of the reader's imagination. But the real trailblazer for Trumpet, cock extraordinary, is SLAWKENBERGIUS'S TALE, twenty pages of Sterne's treatise on noses.[14] A stranger from the "promontory of NOSES" enters Strasburg, as a sentinel announces he "never saw such a nose in his life." "*Benedicity!*" cries the wife of a trumpeter, " 'tis as long as a trumpet." "Is it not a noble nose?" asks the innkeeper's wife. "There is more of it than in any dozen of the largest noses put together in all Strasburg!" (Every virgin who eyes it will be in jeopardy.)

So Burton's *Anatomy of Melancholy*, the other book narrator is reading, is put to work in the story.[15] William Dillingham cites Burton on "melancholy men" who have "such absurd suppositions, as that they are Kings, Lords, cocks." He also argues that what narrator must defend against is "emasculation." This he does successfully by crowing for himself in the end—if that be success. Emery shows how Burton's treatment of melancholy as a disease with causes, diagnosis, and cure all fit Melville's little fiction.

Diagnosis of the narrator is advanced three centuries beyond Burton by Marvin Fisher, who tries to show that he is a "functioning schizophrenic,"[16] but the psychiatry introduced to establish the claim is not at all persuasive. The "artist" (as Fisher sees the narrator) is now depressed, now wildly elated: why isn't the term manic-depressive? No great matter, as it works out. Critic somehow manages to avoid the sexual emphasis in "Cock-a-Doodle-Doo!" and

14. Laurence Sterne, *The Life and Opinions of Tristram Shandy, Gentleman*, ed. Ian Campbell Ross (Oxford: Clarendon Press, 1983), 196–217.

15. Emery, "The Cocks of Melville's 'Cock-a-Doodle-Doo!' " 93–95; William B. Dillingham, *Melville's Short Fiction: 1853–1856* (Athens: University of Georgia Press, 1977), 61–66.

16. Marvin Fisher, *Going Under: Melville's Short Fiction and the American 1850's* (Baton Rouge: Louisiana State University Press, 1977), 164.

discovers a "transcendental view of art" opposing disagreeable reality. There is no response to what author is plainly up to.

And so a large part of the meaning obviously rests in Trumpet. Q. D. Leavis once complained that no one had figured out why he has that name.[17] Melville probably remembered Sterne's nose big as a trumpet, but was likely thinking of Shakespeare—this time in line with ancient folklore at the start of *Hamlet* (I.i) when the Ghost exits as the cock crows. "I have heard," says Horatio, the "cock, that is the trumpet to the morn, / Doth . . . awake the god of day." (To which Marcellus adds his finest lines, "Some say that ever 'gainst that season comes / Wherein our Saviour's birth is celebrated, / This bird of morning singeth all night long.") It is not the rooster but the cock that figures in symbol, folklore and myth. Melville had used him in "The Doubloon," chapter 99 of *Moby-Dick*, where Ahab sees himself on the coin atop an Andes peak, crowing "proud as Lucifer." Cocks have long been symbols of courage and victory—as of exultation, egotism, warning, fame, lust, the male principle. The cock is sacred to Apollo, Athena, and Æsculapius, to stay at the top of the alphabet. It is a symbol of sun and dawn deities, has power to change into a human, is associated with fertility, Christ, and his nativity (it cried "Christus natus est"). On a tomb the cock signifies resurrection. The story of Alectryon, who betrayed his post by falling asleep and was changed into a cock (like Melville's narrator?) is as old as the *Odyssey* and appears in it (8, 300–366). The cockcry is featured in the Gospels of the New Testament. In all four, Jesus, nearing crucifixion, tells Peter that "before the cock crow," or crow twice, he, Peter, will deny being a disciple. The cock crows, as if to signify the immanent end to earthly life.

But Melville's tale belongs in a special category: with those stories he wrote at Pittsfield in the 1850s which challenged and slipped past the guardians of Victorian taste that ruled the magazines that published him. "The Lightning-Rod Man," "I and My Chimney," and "The Tartarus of Maids" all have "hidden meaning": smuggled symbolism in which the "real meaning" is to be found. Although a sexual

17. Q. D. Leavis, "Melville: The 1853–1856 Phase," *New Perspectives on Melville*, ed. Faith Pullin (Kent, Ohio: Kent State University Press, 1978), 201–2.

element is forecast at its opening by two passionate, tragic trains, "Cock-a-Doodle-Doo!" is exceptional in that its "symbolic meaning" is hidden deadpan so far up front that at times one might look right past it. Or pretend to. From start to finish Melville leans heavily on the Order of the Garter, *honi soit qui mal y pense*, shame on him (not to forget her) who thinks evil of it.

There is more to it. Emery generously informs readers that Melville coined Merrymusk by combining two rivers, the Merrimack and the Musketaquid (Indian for the Concord). Whatever for? He knew well that musk is a sexually attractive male secretion: musk deer, muskrat, musk ox, muskmelon, musk rose, musk turtle. Ishmael squeezing spermaceti on the *Pequod* had said, "for a time I lived as in a musky meadow" (chapter 94). (Musk suits a man with no money and four children.) It is not impossible that Melville knew the word comes via Latin *muscus* from Sanskrit *muska*, testicle or scrotum (from *mus*, "little mouse"). (A surprising parallel shows up in chapter 40 of *The Confidence Man*, "The Story of China Aster," which features a fellow nicknamed "Doleful Dumps"—whose real name is Orchis, New Latin for orchid, from Greek *orkhis*, testicle, for the shape of the root of the plant.)

Cock in the vulgar sense is a very old usage. The *OED* is remiss in tracing it but to 1730. Shakespeare used it; so did translators of Rabelais, another Melville favorite. In "pilkoc" it predates Chaucer; in a poem written just after Chaucer there is a cock with a comb of "reed coral," "& euery nyght he perchit hym / in my ladis chambyr."[18]

But Trumpet is far more than a joke—is indeed an ithyphallic symbol and a source of a level of meaning. This is clear and pointed if unremarked on the narrator's first sight of him, emerging from a thicket of alders—that most resplendent creature that ever blessed the sight of man, standing "haughtily," the "red . . . on his crest alone, which was a mighty and symmetric crest, like unto Hector's helmet" (282). The man had heard cockcrows "—but this one! . . . so self-possessed in its very rapture of exultation—so vast, mounting, swelling, soaring, as if it spurted out from a golden throat"

18. Thomas W. Ross, *Chaucer's Bawdy* (New York: Dutton, 1972), 57–58.

(274). Its effect is also remarkable: "how it set me up again! Right on my pins! Yea, verily on stilts" (279).

Trumpet obtrudes. In English less polite there is an old saying that a tumescent phallus has no conscience. This is the story's "secret motto." Depression fled, narrator is reckless, defiant. The dun who used to terrify him he throws bodily into the countryside. He never pays his debt, piles on it. Dillingham is right, the victory is male potency, which the cock proclaimed. But not after all is done. Immemorial belief in the magical power of the cock, faith in a cure for melancholy—all meaning totters with Trumpet's orgasmic crowing at the deaths of Merrymusks. And at his own death, the "little death" become the big one, followed by the pitiful, cuckoo, human cockcry that ends in senseless oos!

If it is madness the narrator ends in, he was not wholly stable to begin with. But what to make of the rest of this? Rapid fire fatality, Merrymusks rocketing to death seriatim, as if Heaven had just opened; Paul's chiseled revelation that obliteration is triumph; a man turning cock as in some forgotten folktale. Until the end, the story made fiction's sense. Then turned fast to scribble. Transcending reality, events leaped orbit. Fairy tale gone haywire, the blackout is something new, untried, a shot in the dark, very risky. Vision cracks, hallucinates. Things deconstruct, fall to bits. What understanding has been reached explodes.

6

Melville Standing: "I and My Chimney"

> I am tied to th' stake, and I must stand the course.
> —Gloucester, in *King Lear*, III. vii. 54

"I and my chimney, two grey-headed old smokers, reside in the country."[1] So starts the narrator, nameless like other personae in short Melville fictions of the time and place: Pittsfield, Massachusetts, in the mid-1850s, right after the unlike failures of *Moby-Dick* and *Pierre*. He quickly points out that though he always speaks first in relation to his chimney, his chimney in fact precedes him. He does not stand before but behind it. It is huge though truncated—a "rather delicate" matter, a "beheading" by a previous owner. Bloodied but unbowed, it still has "the centre of the house to himself": it is like the narrator, masculine.

Well. The problem is that the proud owner of the brick colossus has a wife, with two daughters in her support, who objects to its "stubborn central locality" right where a "fine entrance-hall ought to be." The girls keep measuring for it. In fact the house has no hall, but many strange doors inside, which could bewilder a guest seeking

---

1. "I and My Chimney," *The Piazza Tales and Other Prose Pieces*, ed. Harrison Hayford, Alma A. MacDougall, and G. Thomas Tanselle et al. (Evanston and Chicago: Northwestern University Press and The Newberry Library, 1987), 352–77. Further citations of this tale will be noted parenthetically in the text as *T*. All quotations from Melville's books are taken from this edition.

his room, and knocking on each one "like London's city guest, the king, at Temple Bar."[2] Midway up the chimney is a closet where "I" keeps wines that ripen in gentle heat—but not wife's eggs, "on account of hatching." She is young, at least in spirit; he has sciatica, sometimes crippling. She is a "natural projector. . . . Her maxim is, Whatever is, is wrong; and what is more, must be altered; and what is still more, must be altered right away" (*T*, 362). He loves old things—Montaigne, cheese, wine, the chimney. She wants him to "abdicate," repudiate the great structure and "retire into some sort of monastery. . . . Indeed, the chimney excepted, I have little authority to lay down" (*T*, 362). One day he encounters mysterious lumber on the premises. "Why, old man, don't you know I am building a new barn?" Finally she wants the chimney abolished in toto. "What!" said he, "the chimney is the one grand permanence of this abode. . . . I can't abolish my back-bone" (*T*, 365).

But in time Mr. Scribe, master-mason, is called in. Led to the cellar, he long contemplated the edifice, and finally said "a most remarkable structure, sir." "Yes," said "I" complacently, "every one says so . . . would you have such a famous chimney abolished?" "I wouldn't have it . . . sir, for a gift." But it could be removed, he added, for five hundred dollars. Later he expressed in writing the architectural conjecture that concealed somewhere in the brick was a "secret closet," probably built for an extraordinary object or "treasure" (*T*, 369).

Narrator thinks of the builder of the house, Captain Dacres his late kinsman. Shipmaster and merchant in the India trade, he was said to have retired with a large fortune, put up the house, and left it heavily mortgaged. Then it passed to the stranger, who razed the roof and chimney—and, had he heard of a hidden treasure would have torn down and rummaged the walls. But when wife hears of the closet "—such an explosion!" No matter, "I" was resolved of one thing: "I and my chimney should not budge." "You *know* there must be a secret closet in this chimney" says his wife. "Secret ash-hole, wife, why don't you have it? . . . for where do all the ashes go?" (*T*,

2. The Bar was the gateway to the City of London; long ago the King was not allowed to enter without the Lord Mayor's permission.

372). He will, though, invite Scribe to see if he can find some sign of a hidden space. Paid for a useless effort the mason is bribed into certifying that he found no evidence of a secret closet. The certificate, framed, is hung over the fireplace. Wife and daughters continue tapping the walls with a geological hammer.

Narrator has another objection, and it is earnest: "even if there were a secret closet, secret it should remain. . . . Infinite sad mischief has resulted from the profane bursting open of secret recesses . . . if it have [one] it is my kinsman's. To break into that wall, would be to break into his breast" (*T*, 376). Destructive planning continues. Once, returning early from a city visit, "I" finds three "savages" commencing dismantlement. It is now seven years since he has stirred from home. "I am simply standing guard. . . . I and my chimney will never surrender" (*T*, 377).

An agreeable tale, albeit a man's. But very little agreement as to interpretation. Biographical readings began in 1941 with Merton M. Sealts, Jr.[3] For him the chimney is the "heart and soul" of Melville himself. Scribe's close examination of it he takes to reflect an examination of the author's mental health by Dr. Oliver Wendell Holmes, a neighbor-writer (scribe). Like the "sacred" deceased father in *Pierre*, Dacres is Melville's father—the clincher being that "Dacres" is "simply an anagram for *sacred!*" (Sealts, 18). In 1967, on reconsideration, the critic concedes that only "family tradition" says that Holmes examined Melville's mind. (The family *had* been worrying about his mental health,[4] and the doctor did treat him for sciatica in June 1855, during which time "I and My Chimney" was in progress.)

Lea Newman has published a full and reliable account of the history of an argument that began fifty years ago over the proper reading of this tale.[5] And so it should do here to describe the bounds of contention. Support for Sealts' belief that the story grew out of the

3. See his *Pursuing Melville, 1940–1980* (Madison: University of Wisconsin Press, 1982), 11–22, 171–92.

4. Jay Leyda, *The Melville Log*, 2 vols. (New York: Harcourt, Brace & Co., 1951), 468–69.

5. See her *Reader's Guide to the Short Stories of Herman Melville* (Boston: G. K. Hall, 1986), 229–54.

author's own experience is ample. The chimney is clearly the one at Arrowhead; a recently surfaced letter written by Melville's sister Augusta on moving with his family into that homestead confirms the identification. "Our old farm house," she writes a family friend in 1850, "is built after that peculiarly quaint style of architecture which places the chimney—the hugest in proportions—immediately in the centre, & the rooms around it. An arrangement so totally devoid of grace & beauty. . . ."[6] "We have all sorts of little closets, in all sorts of odd little places," she adds. (A "broad chimney" and the ballustrade that surrounded it had been taken down at Broadhall, the neighboring mansion Herman had known since boyhood; the cellar described in "Chimney" was also Broadhall's.) Elizabeth Melville, Herman's widow, unequivocally identified the narrator with her husband, and remarked pointedly that "All this about his wife applied to his mother—who was very vigorous and energetic about the farm, etc." Removal of the central chimney was "mythical" (T, 716), and just as well.

Ms. Newman summarizes supporters of the "biographically based interpretations" (Newman, 243), a couple of whom move ahead. William G. Crowley sees that preserving the chimney symbolized for Melville the survival of his talent.[7] Vida K. and O. M. Brack depict the narrator "turned at bay" to protect that talent and go on writing, despite great domestic pressure to back off.[8]

These readings have biographical support, but "revisionist" positions sprung up anyway. These go to the heart of the "orthodox" view by rejecting the identification of the author with his symbol. This move opened a large door. Stuart Woodruff considers the tale a symbolic expression of Melville's epistemology—a naturalistic perception of knowledge—and the chimney as a symbol of the "empirical reality of time and its manifestation as history."[9] The door opens wider. William Sowder thinks the chimney a symbol of Negro slavery,

6. Augusta Melville to Mary Blatchford, October 17, 1859. News & Notes: Berkshire County Historical Society 25 (September–October 1990): unpaginated.

7. "Melville's Chimney," Emerson Society Quarterly 14 (1959): 2–6.

8. Vida K. Brack and O. M. Brack, "Weathering Cape Horn: Survivors in Melville's Minor Short Fiction," Arizona Quarterly 28 (1972): 61–73.

9. "Melville and His Chimney," PMLA 75 (1960): 283–92.

foundation of the South's economy, views Scribe as a shady liberal democrat—and the wife of course as an abolitionist.[10] Allan Moore Emery opens it all the way: the narrator is Daniel Webster, arch-conservative, and the framed certificate Scribe produced is the Fugitive Slave Law.[11] There are religious as well as political readings (Newman, 248–49), and an ironic one based on the notion that "I" is a "study in stupidity" (ibid., 247).

What significantly remain are "Freudian analyses," which the *Guide* tends to find "reductive." It may indeed be reductive to "note," as does Martin L. Pops, "covert phallicism" in "Chimney."[12] Nothing about it seems covert to Darwin T. Turner, for whom the story's dominant image is phallic.[13] Failure to see this is to miss much of the whole point. From the start the chimney goes before the narrator, who stands behind it. It "breaks water . . . like an anvil-headed whale"—in *Moby-Dick* called "The Battering Ram." Failure also means missing the whole point of a funny little scene, as critics have generally done, where narrator is caught in his cellar digging the dirt around his symbol. ("I was a little out of my mind, I now think," he says, having no reason but the joke for doing this.) An unexpected neighbor remarks:

> "Ah, loosening the soil, to make it grow. Your chimney, sir, you regard as too small; needing further development, especially at the top?"
>
> "Sir!" said I . . . "do not be personal. I and my chimney—"
>
> "Personal?"
>
> (*T*, 358)

It hatches his wife's eggs. In her *Feminization of American Culture* Ann Douglas has something to add.[14] The chimney is a "bastion of

10. "Melville's 'I and My Chimney': A Southern Exposure," *Mississippi Quarterly* 16 (1963): 128–45.

11. "The Political Significance of Melville's Chimney," *New England Quarterly* 55 (1982): 201–28.

12. *The Melville Archetype* (Kent, Ohio: Kent State University Press, 1970), 174.

13. "Smoke from Melville's Chimney," *College Language Association Journal* 7 (1963): 107–13.

14. (New York: Alfred A. Knopf, 1977), 384.

phallic, assertive, and aggressive masculinity"—but it contains "womb imagery": the sealed inner space with a treasure (that is, a child) in it. This feminizes matters (if the hidden place exists). Newman on her own claims that in the end the narrator is fighting a "losing battle" (250). She also points out that after "Bartleby" and "Benito" "Chimney" is the Melville tale "most written about."

All the harder to explain why significant features of the story have never really been looked into. One of these is the offstage character, important to the narrator, his kinsman Captain Julian Dacres. The name is not "sacred"; Melville punned, but did not do anagrams. The man was first identified (only) by William Dillingham[15] as in life Captain James Dacres, once-famous commander of the *Guerrière*, spectacularly defeated in the War of 1812 by the *Constitution*. He had recently come to attention on his death in 1853 (and Arrowhead had been built by a Captain, David Bush). Why Melville should relate his kinsman/father to an English naval officer can perhaps be explained. Herman's father used to entertain him and his brother Gansevoort with "stories of his travels."[16] An exciting event would have taken place in 1811, when as an importer at sea his ship was captured by the *Guerrière* (Gilman, 300 n. 151). The boy also enjoyed trips to his grandfather in Boston, where Major Thomas displayed his Revolutionary relics (ibid., 38). When the renowned British frigate with the French name was taken by "Old Ironsides," Dacres was put aboard, carried to Boston, and paroled there.[17] The Collector of the Port at that time was Major Melvill, who would not have forgot the loser of a fabled engagement.

Realization that the narrator's kinsman represents Melville's father is over forty years old. By now it should have thrown powerful light on just what "I" had in mind when he warned emotionally of the damage that revealing a man's secret can do. But has not. Melville's knowledge was born of painful experience, most directly related in

15. *Melville's Short Fiction, 1853–1856* (Athens: University of Georgia Press, 1977), 284 n. 20.

16. William H. Gilman, *Melville's Early Life and "Redburn"* (New York: New York University Press, 1951), 35.

17. *Appleton's Cyclopædia of American Biography*, ed. J. G. Wilson and J. Fiske (New York: D. Appleton and Company, 1888), 2:52.

Pierre in 1852. There the protagonist—like the narrator of "Chimney," a thin disguise for the author—learned young that his deceased father, whom he had equated with deity, had sired a never-acknowledged daughter. This fact had brought about the "infinite sad mischief" that "I" warns of: it had ultimately destroyed Pierre. As for the "profane bursting open" of private secrets, Melville had done something of the sort in publishing *Pierre*; as he would soon discover, the book ruined what was left of his reputation as a writer.

Something less telling but far more obvious appears to have escaped notice in the very many readings of "I and My Chimney": that a substantial part of the story is Melville's version of a piece of Gothic machinery Hawthorne had put to heavier use in his *House of the Seven Gables*—which the author presented to Melville on April 11, 1851 (and which the recipient praised extravagantly in a letter of thanks five days later) (Leyda, *The Melville Log*, 1:409–10). Like Arrowhead, the great house in Salem had in its very "midst" a "huge" chimney; a kinsman had died leaving a fortune that could not be located; this ancestor, a Colonel, builder of the house, had expired after signing a treaty by which he had bought vast tracts of land from Indians; the ancient deed to them drops from its hiding place in a recess in a wall, hidden behind the builder's portrait.

After Dacres, the important unexplored figure in "Chimney" is Saint Dunstan (and his devil). Melville obvious enjoyed tucking improper jokes into tales like this one. But in this one he risked offending what is still considered good taste by many. And this is presumably one reason at least why the author's meaning has not been much looked into when narrator asked wife a second time about the matter: "What devil, wife, prompted you to crawl into the ashhole! Don't you know that St. Dunstan's devil emerged from the ashhole?" (*T*, 372).

Saint and Devil together pose no problem here. It is a very old story, often summarized in a picture, that Saint Dunstan (c. 909–88), eventually Archbishop of Canterbury, had been a goldsmith and once got the devil by the nose with his pincers and banished him. (Melville referred to "St. Dunstan's long tongs" in *Pierre* [207].) A sign depicting the scene hung outside "The Devil and St. Dunstan's," a famous Elizabethan tavern next to London's Temple Bar, close by

St. Dunstan's Church, which site Melville visited on November 18, 1849.[18] The "hole" narrator refers to is from an equally old story. According to his biographer,[19] Dunstan at Glastonbury was himself (not his devil) thrown from the King's palace by enemies, beaten, and tossed into a "bog," from which *he* emerged "covered with filth." In legend the bog became, or perhaps originally was, a "filthy pit"[20] or cesspool—a story Melville may have heard at the Church or read in one of the guides to or other books on London. Narrator conflates the two stories of Dunstan.

The fundamental hole at the base of the chimney is at the bottom of another bit of private play that gets overlooked when the narrator introduces himself (*T*, 353) as one in a "sad rearward way," "running behindhand." He is unlike his forehanded neighbors, among whom there are rumors of his "behindhandedness," which are true. Returning to his personal chimney in a similar spirit (353), he remarks that though he much ministers to it, never does it minister or incline over to him but "rather leans the other way" (somewhat as the gentleman's bespoke tailor, arrived at the trousers, asks "dress left or right, sir?").

All this is play, which may distract from the life-and-death seriousness of author and narrator in determining never to give up a chimney. It meant, to Melville, life itself, his existence as a writer, which is what he was. To abdicate would mean bowing to the serious pressure—exerted for the sake of his uncertain health—of wife, mother, and influential friends to give up his unrelenting compulsion to go on. William Crowley and the Bracks were on target. There was to boot real interior pressure: like Pierre, Melville knew well his "hereditary liability to madness" (*Pierre*, 287). Father and older brother were said to have died insane and early. (After *Pierre* he was himself called "crazy" in print.) Wife and mother were as determined as he to break off his losing battle to achieve recognition already due him—by getting him not to a monastery but to a consulate such as

18. Herman Melville, *Journals*, ed. Howard C. Horsford with Lynn Horth (Evanston and Chicago: Northwestern University Press and The Newberry Library, 1989), 20.

19. Eleanor Shipley Duckett, *Saint Dunstan of Canterbury* (New York: Norton, 1955), 39–40.

20. *Catholic Encyclopedia* (New York: Encyclopedia Press, 1913), 5:199–202.

Hawthorne now occupied. The cause was pressed on two presidents, Pierce and Lincoln (*The Melville Log*, 1:468–74; 2:635). In vain.

But it is not clear in the end that narrator is "fighting a losing battle" to protect his chimney and all it "stands for." Just how much that is lies at the heart of the debate over the story's meaning. It is the narrator who said the chimney was what "little authority" he had to lay down. It was D. H. Lawrence who expressed fully and bluntly what this means, and there is no better symbol for it than Melville's. Lawrence's term was "ithyphallic authority" (Greek *ithu*, erect). "True male authority," he went on in *Studies in Classic American Literature*, "masterhood."[21] "I and My Chimney" is a "phallocentric text" if there ever was one.

Worse health and the impossibility of supporting an extended family by writing for an audience that was not really there eventually forced Melville from Arrowhead to New York, where in total obscurity and infirmity he continued writing, was still not done with *Billy Budd* when he died. An excellent sense of the audience that was not there can be got from a news item of later date that Jay Leyda dug up in the files of the *New York Times*, October 10, 1937:

MELVILLE'S CHIMNEY INTACT IN OLD HOUSE
*Author of 'Moby Dick' Refused
to Remove Fireplace Built in
1780 on Pittsfield Estate*

"Fireplace." A new sale of Arrowhead inspired this release. Reporter explains that details of his account are taken from "I and My Chimney," Melville's "essay." *Essay*. It would have bewildered a reader of this to learn that before very long there would be those for whom the pre-Churchillian ring of "I and my chimney will never surrender" would mean something. Narrator in self-defense had told his wife, "When all this house shall have crumbled from it, the chimney will still survive—a Bunker Hill monument." What author never knew was that if Arrowhead should burn to the ground its chimney would remain his monument.

21. (Garden City, N.Y.: Doubleday, Anchor, 1953), 109. These terms appear in a chapter on *The Scarlet Letter*.

7

The Machine in Tartarus: Melville's *Inferno*

"The Paradise of Bachelors and the Tartarus of Maids" is Melville's title.[1] He could have got separate if unequal pieces out of the material. Perhaps he should have, since relationship between the parts rests chiefly in dissimilarity, even opposition. "Opposites attract," but here neither side is drawn to the other; sex is unexercised or atrophied. It is true that overfed or unfed Bachelors and Maids are equally sterile and that the segments do share an unnamed narrator. Melville is attempting what is called a diptych, after an ancient writing tablet having two hinged panels. Of his three tries with the form this is the best, though the hinge might be better oiled. And "The Tartarus of Maids" might command more attention if it stood alone.

"Paradise" is set in the "stony heart of stunning London," where a "cool, deep" shady glen is monastically cloistered from the care-worn world. To appreciate the place you would have to dine there at the invitation of some Templar. Templar? Knights Templars? "We know indeed . . . that a moral blight tainted at last this sacred Brotherhood. . . . The genuine Templar is long since departed." But the ancient buildings and grounds and the nominal society remain. The Templar is a lawyer—also a bachelor and "capital diner." The narrator's host is such.

Nine men sat at dinner, which was hearty and heady with innumerable dishes, wines, and "silver flagons of humming ale." State

---

1. *The Piazza Tales and Other Prose Pieces, 1839–1860*, ed. Harrison Hayford, Alma A. MacDougall, and G. Thomas Tanselle et al. (Evanston and Chicago: Northwestern University Press and The Newberry Library, 1987), 316–35. Further citations will be noted parenthetically in the text as *T*.

bumpers, impromptu glasses between, elaborate courtesies, convivial if formalized conversation, pleasant stories told betimes. No wives or children. At the end arrives an immense horn containing "some choice Rappee . . . a mull of snuff." Finally, arm in arm, the men descend and part, some to "turn over the Decameron ere retiring." Narrator is "last lingerer." "Sir," he says to his smiling host, "Sir, this is the very Paradise of Bachelors!"

So Melville first called it in his journal for 20 December 1849, having enjoyed a glorious dinner at Elm Court, Temple. He had already visited Temple Church for the music, and seen the nine effigies of Crusaders who had been to the Holy Land. Next day he wrote, "Last night dined at the Erechtheum Club St: James's . . . nine sat down—fine dinner. . . . An exceedingly agreeable company. The 'Mull' after dinner."[2] Perhaps the ennead at table pleased him; there were originally nine Knights Templars.

"Paradise" is more nearly an informal essay than a tale. Its bursting geniality is not characteristic of Melville, and there is little substance. Ritualized dining appears somewhat empty. The fact is that when the author experienced the London dinners he was terribly homesick for wife and infant child Malcolm (J, 17, 25, 31, passim). Perhaps because there is so little to the sketch, attention has fixed on the taint of "moral blight" that nibbled at "the monastic vow." Sacrilege and sodomy were among the accusations made centuries ago; the subject was controversial in Melville's day. Perhaps as a result, sexual signs and symbols have been discovered all over the place. Browsing in the Decameron is autoerotic activity; the mull is a vagina; the great horn that contains it can go sexually either way. The deep glen where Paradise is to be found is "a symbolic anus"; the snuff that diners insert in their mouths is "aromatic sperm."[3] Such striking insights might better suit the second half of the diptych. But "The Tartarus of Maids," nothing like an essay, is an extraordinary, underrated performance, itself in two parts.

2. *Journals*, ed. Howard C. Horsford with Lynn Horth (Evanston and Chicago: Northwestern University Press and The Newberry Library, 1989), 45. Further citations will be noted parenthetically in the text as *J*.

3. Robyn Wiegman, "Melville's Geography of Gender," *American Literary History* 1 (1989): 738, 740.

Even left to stand alone, however, it will remain underrated until important matters are better understood. First the tale itself needs rehearsing, so that details emerge as leads to scarcely explored levels of classical myth and Christian allegory. An exciting new friend of the early days of Melville's marriage must be introduced as the all but certain source of an elaborate symbol which is the goal of a memorable journey. Awareness of a feature of the author's married life at Pittsfield during 1853–54 when "Tartarus" was written should explain its unexpected meaning. The point of his story, clearly stated but obscured by critics who infer a protest he never made, should be plain.

I

Melville is magic. Not far from Woedolor Mountain in New England begins a wild excursion. A traveler, down in a pung by a powerful horse, enters bleak hills which close on a dusky pass, where a violent stream of air drives between "cloven walls of haggard rock." This is called the "Mad Maid's Bellows'-pipe." At the bottom of a gorge, steep walls contract at a point known as the Black Notch. The ravine, descending, expands into a "great, purple, hopper-shaped hollow" sunk among "shaggy-wooded mountains" and locally referred to as the Devil's Dungeon. Torrents on all sides unite in "one turbid brick-colored stream, boiling through a flume" and named Blood River. Near the bottom of the Dungeon like a "whited sepulchre" is a papermill. The narrating traveler is in "the seedsman's business." Mailing seeds over a large area requires an "incredible quantity" of paper, and—heavily robed in furs against bitter January cold—he has come by sleigh to order it. Intense "congelation" has the whole region looking petrified. More like frozen glass, the very snow is icy. Forests "strangely groaned" with cold. Black, the good horse, runs at terrific speed, "flaked all over with frozen sweat." At Bellows' Pipe the blast "shrieked"; the animal "slung out," swept grazingly through the narrow notch and downward, rushed into the Dungeon with the cataract.

Mountains stood "pinned in shrouds." And "there, like an arrested avalanche," was the white-washed factory. Beside the main building, Blood River "demoniacally boiled." Thin apron over head, a girl ran from a doorway. The driver hailed her to ask about a shed for Black. She turned a pale face upon him and was silent. In a moment it was the same with another girl. Then a well-wrapped, dark-complexioned man passed and directed him to the woodshed, where he blanketed the horse, piling buffalo robes on top.

Inside were rows of windows where blank-looking girls folded blank paper blankly. A "vertical thing like a piston" was periodically rising and falling. The hum of "iron animals" was the only sound, the girls "mere cogs to the wheels." Suddenly the dark man cried out, seized his arm, dragged him into the open, grabbed some congealed snow, and began rubbing his face: "man, your cheeks are frozen." A "tearing pain" hit them as they came to life. "Two gaunt blood-hounds . . . seemed mumbling them. I seemed Actæon." Back inside he asked to see the factory, and—red-cheeked and spirited-looking— the boy Cupid was summoned as guide.

The "dark colossal water-wheel, grim with its one immutable purpose," came first. The waters of Blood River, noticed the seeds-man, had not changed color. They run the whole machine, said Cupid. Up a rickety stair in a light room were "manger-like receptacles" with rows of girls like haltered mares before them. In front of each stood a glittering scythe, across which each Maid forever dragged strips of washed rags, rendering tatter almost to lint.

Before the great machine that makes the paper was a "bespattered place, with two great round vats in it, full of a white, wet, woolly-looking stuff, not unlike the albuminous part of an egg, soft-boiled." Here the "first beginnings of the paper," pouring from both vats into a common channel headed for the machine. Then a room, "stifling" with "blood-like abdominal heat," where "germinous particles" just seen are developed. Here is a length of "iron frame-work—multitudinous and mystical, with all sorts of rollers, wheels, and cylinders, in slowly-measured and unceasing motion."

For a while the pulp is "quite delicate and defective"; farther on it becomes "something you might possibly handle in the end." It must take a long time to come out paper, says the man. "Oh!" smiles

Cupid, "only nine minutes." And it was no longer when the man saw a "sort of paper-fall," and a "scissory sound smote my ear, as of some cord being snapped; and down dropped an unfolded sheet of perfect foolscap." Watch in hand he reports, "Nine minutes to a second." Astonishing. Yet "terrible" the "metallic necessity, the unbudging fatality," the "unvarying docility" of the product to its manufacture.

But he kept watching. In the "pallid incipience of the pulp" he seemed to make out the "yet more pallid faces of all the pallid girls," as beseechingly, yet unresistingly, they gleamed along. "Halloa!" Cupid cried, staring—"the heat of the room is too much for you." Hurried again outdoors, then a little revived, the visitor went to transact his business with Old Bach, as the dark man is secretly known to the girls (he's a bachelor). "Your machine," said the seedsman, "is a miracle of inscrutable intricacy. . . . Why is it, Sir, that in most factories, female operatives" are called "girls, never women?" Probably because they are unmarried; married women are "apt to be off-and-on too much." Then these are all maids, said the seedsman. "All maids. . . . Your cheeks look whitish yet, Sir . . . be careful going home . . . it is colder here than at the top of Woedolor Mountain." Black is doubled up. In the pung the narrator, wrapped "in furs and meditations," ascends from the Dungeon, pauses at Black Notch, and shoots the pass—along, as he says, with inscrutable nature.

Unique, substantial, "Tartarus" is one of Melville's most remarkable tales. Even on a literal level the trip to the mill is brilliant. "Nothing could be finer," writes Newton Arvin, than its wintry landscape.[4] Stark, graphic in black and white, electric, strange, it hints of the reckless inner landscape of the sleighman. The voyeur in the mill is a bold invention, like nothing of its time and place. Neither part of the story has been really explored.

II

Since "Tartarus" was plainly unprintable, it is a tribute to Melville that he wrote it anyway, and a tribute to people at *Harper's New*

4. *Herman Melville* (New York: William Sloane, 1950), 238.

Monthly and its readers that they were sufficiently blind (or embarrassed) to remain silent when it appeared in April 1855. (There seems to be no record of any response.) Exposed to the symbolism, modern readers would (once, at any rate) think of Freud. Or, in the way of fiction, of Kafka, specifically of "In the Penal Colony," which it startlingly resembles in the way of machinery. No matter that Melville's story was published in the year before Freud was born. Or that the "Penal Colony" appeared when the American was thirty years in Woodlawn Cemetery. "Tartarus" is protomodernist Melville. Eco caught up with him in *Foucault's Pendulum*: "And now you see the beauty of the idea . . . the chthonic uterus" (504).

How he got away with it for some readers, anyway, is probably explained by Lea Newman: Loose parallels between the seedsman's route and local geography, and similarities in nomenclature, "were apparently sufficiently striking to convince contemporaneous readers that Melville's sketch [*sic*] was primarily a travel account!"⁵ These readers are matched in our time by critics who manage to read the story sociologically. Little can be done (unless by psychiatry) for the few who have claimed there *is* no "gestation symbolism" in "Tartarus." Those who have missed it can be helped. The problem is with those who understand well enough and continue to think that the tale is essentially a Melvillean denunciation of the industrial revolution. In his book on the author, Michael Paul Rogin, an informed and perceptive reader, still calls the tale a "sketch [*sic*] of working-class life," and assigns it to his chapter on "Class Struggles in America."⁶ Ray B. Browne, who understands the symbolism just as well, calls it a "cry for improved working conditions"—Melville's "anguished protest rings out."⁷ Such critics respond to a story Melville did not write.

As for gestation symbolism, readers who never got to *The Interpretation of Dreams* should pick it up before long. The Black Notch is arresting, if not seductive; as it expands into a Hopper run by Blood

5. *A Reader's Guide to the Short Stories of Herman Melville* (Boston: G. K. Hall, 1986), 287.

6. *Subversive Genealogy: The Politics and Art of Herman Melville* (Berkeley and Los Angeles: University of California Press, 1983), 201–4.

7. *Melville's Drive to Humanism* (Lafayette, Ind.: Purdue University Studies, 1971), 227.

River, meaning appears inescapable. After a rising and falling piston, vats of wet white stuff, and so forth, things end explicitly in the cutting of a cord.

The question of how far to take some things is debatable. A seedsman wanting envelopes in which to dispatch seeds certainly suggests contraception. Black, "sweeping grazingly through the narrow notch," has been perceived as phallic. So his passenger, finding himself "silently and privily stealing through deepcloven passages" into the "sequestered spot" where the factory is located, thinks of the "marvelous retirement of this mysterious mountain nook" (suggesting "nooky," a low noun? Melville liked to do this sort of thing). On the other hand, repeated interpretation of the scythes before the Maids as *vagina dentata* is forced; the girls are not attractive in the first place. (Indeed each sword, "its edge turned outward," suggests if anything phallic rejection.) Critical control is healthy. When the narrator asks on behalf of his horse, "is there no shed hereabouts which I may drive into?" a recent response, "Women, like sheds, function as sheaths for the phallus,"[8] seems gratuitous.

What seems nonsense is that the mythic Greek Actæon, whom the narrator felt like for a moment, is "the typical folk-figure . . . a huntsman, accompanied by two dogs, exemplifying coitus."[9] Several interpreters take the intense cold at the Dungeon to stand "both for male impotence and for man's association with women as the narrator sees it." What follows from this is ridiculous: his "repugnance for the inexorable nature of sex [not 'reproduction'] . . . turns the whole world of women [Tarts?] into a brothel and lying-in hospital simultaneously" (Rowland, 170). Credit for calling the papermill a "labor-saving device" goes to Larzer Ziff.[10]

Newman's reference to geography and place names is on target. Late in January, when the tale is set, Melville did drive (in 1851) to Carson's "Old Red Mill" to get "a sleigh-load of paper."[11] It was

---

8. Wiegman, "Melville's Geography of Gender," 742–43.

9. Beryl Rowland, "Melville's Bachelors and Maids: Interpretation Through Symbol and Metaphor," in *On Melville: The Best from* American Literature, ed. Louis J. Budd and Edwin H. Cady (Durham: Duke University Press, 1988), 168.

10. *Literary Democracy* (New York: Viking, 1981), 293.

11. Jay Leyda, *The Melville Log*, 2 vols. (New York: Harcourt, Brace & Co., 1951), 1:403. Further citations will be noted parenthetically in the text as *L*.

"about five miles from here [Pittsfield]," he wrote Evert Duyckinck on a sheet of it. In August of that summer Duyckinck wrote his wife about his own "ascent of Saddleback" (another name for Greylock), the "highest mountain in Massachusetts." He was in a party of twelve, which included Melville and his sister Augusta. (Lizzie, Melville's wife, was home pregnant as it turned out with Stanwix, their second child.) We did it, Duyckinck continues, with "four horses in a four seated wagon. . . . Ascending you get to a passage . . . 'the Bellows Pipe' or 'Notch' pass. . . . Then you have the ascent proper . . . *three* miles of the toughest bog and stumbling which could well be got up by the forces of mountain torrents, the rotting of mists, snows, and ever falling vegetation." Later: "The Fire. It is dark. Melville's axe is ringing against the fallen trees lying about and with the fireplace among the roots of a huge decaying stump . . . fanned by the wind. . . . The ladies are lying around in buffalo robes borrowed from the sleighing parties of last winter" (*L*, 1:423–24). Next morning, "descending, you are in the midst of closely fitting mountains—a grand neighborhood. A part of these descending form the 'Hopper' a deep valley with clean descending mountain sides in the shape of that household implement" (*T*, 711).[12]

Augusta Melville recorded no less than six "Berkshire excursions" made by Melville, family, and others in the spring of 1852.[13] It is revealing of the seedsman's ride in "Tartarus" that ten years later (1862) Melville's friend and early biographer J. E. A. Smith of Pittsfield testified that "on mountain excursions" the author was "a driver daring to the point of recklessness"—and of "sometimes terrified passengers." He had, in November, had a bad accident in his wagon,

12. Vividly conveying vertical data, the topographic U.S. Geological Survey Map called "Williamstown Quadrangle, Massachusetts-Vermont," 1973, prominently shows the Hopper, so labeled, with Hopper Brook, Trail, and Road, as well as the Bellows Pipe and Bellows Pipe Trail (newly called Ski Trail) and, beside the Pipe, Notch Brook, which runs into Notch Reservoir. The "strangely ebon hue" of the steep walls of Melville's Black Notch appears as a sharply inclined area known as Raven Rocks. In August 1990 a landslide scarred the western slope of Greylock. Foresters hiked in to examine the damage in "an isolated and federally protected glen called 'The Hopper,' " which contains "some of the last virgin spruce forest in New England." (Apparently the trees, over 300 years old, were spared.) *Boston Globe*, 10 August 1990, 19.

13. Merton M. Sealts, Jr., "Melville in the Spring of 1852," *Melville Society Extracts* 79 (November 1989): 1–3.

"and for a time shrank from entering a carriage." It was "doubtful," Smith thought, that he ever overcame the shock (*L*, 2:655–56). Back in the summer of 1853 when he began the story, Melville climbed the mountain. His third child Elizabeth had been born in May. As for the topography and nomenclature of the trip to the papermill, Emerson had said it in *Nature* (1836): "there is a radical correspondence between visible things and human thoughts."

III

But a little lower level of "Tartarus" broadens the meanings. As soon as the second paragraph a directional signal goes up: the Hopper is sunk among "Plutonian mountains." A book as familiar as *The Age of Fable*, a compendium first published in the year of the story by Thomas Bulfinch, gives an easy start. In the myth of Proserpine, the Titans had been banished to Tartarus—underworld as deep below as heaven above. Giants buried alive under Mount Ætna so shook the earth that Pluto, "dark monarch" of this hell, alarmed that his kingdom be exposed to light, mounted his chariot drawn by black horses, and took off to inspect the place. In his sleigh, drawn by a proper horse, Melville's traveler finds Pluto on the job in the dark Bach—like Pluto a harsh superintendent, not himself a judge or tormentor, and a bachelor. In the myth of Proserpine, Venus had sent Cupid to put a dart in Pluto's breast, asking "why should he alone escape?" In Melville's underworld, the boy is dartless. A cruel presence as he glides through "passive-looking girls—like a gold fish through hueless waves," says the narrator, he is "doing nothing . . . that I could see."

A partial precedent for Melville's Blood River lies in the fiery-red waters of the river Phlegethon in Hades. Putting the stream to productive use was quite probably the author's idea, but the concept may also have been ancient, if difficult to verify.[14] As for Styx, it

---

14. According to Barbara G. Walker's *Woman's Encyclopedia of Myths and Secrets* (San Francisco: Harper & Row, 1983), 639, "Greek mystics were 'born again' out of the river Styx, which wound seven times through the earth's interior and emerged at a yonic shrine near the city of Clitor (Greek *Kleitoris*). . . . Styx was the blood-stream from the earth's vagina."

translates "hateful, gloomy." In later times it was identified with a stream called Mavronéri (Greek: Black Water), located in the mountains of Arcadia. (Thackeray wrote "as black as Styx"—*Esmond*.) In Dante the Styx is a swamp, though it contains a well of "inky waters" (vii, 108). In *The White Goddess* (1952, 365) Robert Graves quotes the ancient account of one Pausanias which mentions a shrine of the Barley Mother at Clitor. He also reports that Sir James Frazer, visiting the area in 1895, remarked the overhanging gorge of Styx, the waters appearing black as they ran down cliffsides of dark rock—like the walls of "ebon hue" (Raven) at Black Notch. A bloody river in hell is mentioned in *Paradise Lost* (i, 450–52).

Bulfinch describes Actæon with dogs after him in a chase "swifter than the wind. Over rocks and cliffs, through the mountain gorges that seemed impracticable." So the speeding sleighman already "seemed Actæon" before he got to Tartarus. The huntsman's misfortune was of course to have glimpsed the virgin queen at her bath, and as a result he was torn apart by the hunting dogs that caught him. Similarly the seedsman was about to "see too much," the inner workings of gestation, when his cheeks were savaged.

Before descending into the Dungeon early in "Tartarus," you stand "as within a Dantean gateway"—or frame of reference. Except for visitors, passing through it means abandoning hope. Purchased for Melville's account on 22 June 1848 was "1 Cary's Dante, $2.12." (On 10 November 1989 Sotheby's sold this copy, "heavily annotated," for $20,000.) The Reverend Henry Francis Cary's translation, once very widely read, was published in London a year before Melville acquired it. Next year, on his first visit to London, he was already seeing through Dante's eyes: the place appeared "a city of Dis (Dante's) clouds of smoke—the damned &c—coal barges—coaly waters . . . its marks are left upon you, &c &c &c" (*J*, 14). He called the Thames "the muddy Phlegthon" (*T*, 311).

Phlegethon came to Dante via Virgil from myths of an infernal river of fire, which Dante turned to boiling blood, the blood of sinners who had shed it on earth. Twice he pictures it boiling (forms of "bolle"), which Cary changes to "steeped" and "seething." It is not known that Melville ever saw the *Inferno* in Italian, but his instincts were with Dante's: he brings blood back to the boil ("boiling through a flume," "redly and demoniacally boiled").

There is a hint of Dante, at least by hindsight, in the first line of "Tartarus," when Mount Greylock is somewhat awkwardly and redundantly called "Woedolor," which does quite suit the *Inferno*. At his famed gate the poet uses forms of "dolor" (*dolente, dolore*); Acheron, across which Charon ferries souls of the dead, meant "stream of woe." When Melville's narrator hears how the frozen forest "strangely groaned" and the gust "shrieked . . . as if laden with lost spirits bound to the unhappy world," the *Inferno* is close by.

Dante at the start, like the seedsman, soon finds himself in a "savage wild" forest which quickly leads to a "mountain's foot . . . where closed / The valley that had pierced my heart with dread." The tension that grips the Melville journey charges Dante's: "my spirit . . . struggling with terror" had scarce begun the ascent "when lo! a panther." Then, a "new dread," a lion "hunger-mad," then a she-wolf. (In Jeremiah 5:6 it's a lion, a wolf, and a leopard—and "every one that goeth out thence shall be torn in pieces.") With Melville it's a fallen distorted hemlock, "darkly undulatory as an anaconda," then a rock "couchant as a lion in the way." When Dante got to Charon collecting the spirits "faint and naked," he lost consciousness.

Hell is commonly associated with fire, infernos with fiery furnaces, holocaust. So in the *Inferno* at the end of Canto IX, where Dante enters "The City of Dis" (title of a powerful short chapter on London in Melville's *Israel Potter*, published the same year as "Tartarus"). (In Dante the very graves are afire.) The preternatural cold at the Devil's Dungeon could reflect the fact that both author and narrator traveled there in a Berkshire January. But what Melville had clearly in mind were Cantos XXXII–XXXIV of the *Inferno*, set in the ninth and lowest circle of hell, the "frozen circle." As he knew, Milton's hell in *Paradise Lost* (II, 599–602) adopted the concept of "fierce extremes . . . / From beds of raging fire to starve in ice . . . infixed and frozen round," which is ancient.[15] Dante found underfoot a lake of glass,

---

15. The idea can be found in *The Apocryphal Old Testament*, ed. H.F.D. Sparks (Oxford: Clarendon Press, 1984), 331–32, in 2 Enoch 5:11–13, where "to the north of the heaven" is a

toward which the ninth circle sloped in the shape of a funnel (a hopper is a large funnel). The seedsman saw that the snow was glassy ("vitreous," Melville wrote; Dante wrote *vetro*). Here, says Dante, "Blue pinch'd and shrined in ice the spirits stood. . . . Their eyes express'd the dolour of their heart." Outside the factory, Melville's girls are "blue with cold . . . eye supernatural with unrelated misery." The factory, "frost-painted to a sepulchre," evokes the "whited sepulchres" of Matthew 23:27, "beautiful out- ward, but . . . full of dead men's bones."

The Maids of Tartarus, though spoken to, do not in the tale speak. They are Dante's "shades," which is to say spirits of the dead inhabiting hell. Sentenced to more than maidenhood, they are female counterparts to the sad, silent, lackluster and ultimately dead bow- lers Rip Van Winkle saw in the Catskills. Or they are Melville's version of the first spirits Dante encountered at the entrance to the underworld (Canto III) who, as Virgil explains, "of death / No hope may entertain." This is what Newton Arvin sensed (*Melville*, 238), but could not put his finger on, when he perceived that the Maids were enslaved in some "indirect and enigmatic sense"—which cannot be accounted for without awareness of those sighing souls Eliot pictured in *The Waste Land* as a crowd flowing over London Bridge— "so many, / I had not thought death had undone so many." (Cary wrote, "Such a long train of spirits, I should ne'er / Have thought that death so many had despoil'd.") At Virgil's explanation, Dante passed out. So, when he had seen the factory, Melville's narrator had to be rushed outdoors by *his* guide to revive. Earlier, dragged into the cold by the dark boss to have his cheeks rubbed with congealed snow, he echoed what was demanded of Dante in the same frozen circle (XXXII, 88–89): "Now who art thou . . . smiting others' cheeks . . . with such force?"

IV

When Melville began the Paradise/Tartarus diptych in the late sum- mer of 1853, he had visited London, made the trip to the mill by

---

"very terrible place . . . a river of fire rising up," and "cold and ice and prisons." The root *ndher* from which "inferno" comes means simply "under," as in mythic underworlds.

sleigh and other Berkshire outings, and become a father for the third time. By the time the tale was published, his fourth child (second daughter, Frances) had arrived. Add the *Inferno* plus a little myth, and the sources of "Tartarus" should be apparent. But there was another factor that has never been mentioned.

In the early years after their marriages in 1847, the brothers Herman and Allan Melville and their brides shared a house at 103 Fourth Avenue, New York City, with their mother and four unmarried sisters. The great growth in the ambitions of the writer which took place between *Typee* and *Omoo*, both in print, and *Mardi* was closely related to Herman's burgeoning friendship with Evert Duyckinck. This young man had a library of some 16,000 volumes, some of them "classics," which he was happy to lend a promising younger one. Developing around Duyckinck, further, was a coterie of writers and others who enjoyed literary and political conversation, a few of them physicians. One, a friend of the young Melvilles, was Dr. John W. Francis, at some point Professor of Obstetrics at Columbia.

"Perhaps the most stimulating of all" Melville's acquaintances at the time, however, was a new friend, Dr. Augustus Kinsley Gardner, a man of literary interests, "a store of curious information, and an original inquisitiveness about medical and other scientific matters." He "kept Melville's mind in a state of excitement."[16] Fresh from studying "obstetrics and lunacy" in Paris, Gardner had written letters home that were published in his father's Newark, New Jersey, newspaper. He had been an energetic, well-educated, curious, and appreciative tourist; the letters appeared as a book called *Old Wine in New Bottles; or, Spare Hours of a Student in Paris* (1848). He inscribed and presented a copy to Melville, who liked it. (It is a much better book than might be expected.)

Gardner's medical career is thoroughly told in five chapters of G. J. Barker-Benfield's frequently horrifying *Horrors of the Half-Known Life* [title from *Moby-Dick*]: *Male Attitudes toward Women and Sexuality in Nineteenth-Century America.*[17] "Obstetrics and lunacy" were coupled in the belief that special liability to insanity in the female

16. Leon Howard, *Herman Melville* (Berkeley and Los Angeles: University of California Press, 1951), 110.

17. (New York: Harper & Row, 1976), 229–95.

rests in the sexual organs. The exception to French leadership in mid-century medicine was in American gynecological surgery; the first successful American hysterectomy was performed in 1853. The "great apostle of vaginal surgery," as his convert Gardner called him, was Dr. J. Marion Sims. But on matters of gestation and parturition it was Gardner who wrote and published regularly. On the descent of women in Paris he had written, "the kept mistress, the courtezan, the street-sweeper, the inmate of the hospital, *the subject of the dissecting room!* But here we leave them—the secrets of another world are not, as yet, unfolded" (*Old Wine*, 46).

Not to laymen. But Gardner tells, for example, of a public dissecting room where 4,000 bodies from Paris hospitals were annually consumed in anatomy instruction (remains fed to dogs). All medical students were observers at midwifery hospitals, especially if surgery was involved. When in Paris, it pleased Melville to stay where Gardner had recommended, at Madame Capelle's in the Latin Quarter. Given Gardner's enthusiasm and specialties it is hard to think he had nothing to do with "Tartarus."

When the Melvilles returned to New York from Pittsfield in 1863, Gardner was their doctor. When in September 1867 Malcolm Melville shot himself in the head, it was Gardner who "advised that the coroner should be called" (*L*, 2:688). As Melville almost certainly never knew, four months prior to this tragedy his wife's family, the Shaws of Boston, had tried to get Lizzie to leave her husband and come to live with them. The reason was Herman's ill treatment of her, and her belief in his insanity, encouraged by her minister Dr. Bellows and "the professional advice of Dr. Gardner."[18] (She resisted, helped him, and survived. Gardner was deceased by the time Melville developed the heart problems he died of.)

Even with the author in good health the strain on a relationship with Gardner could have been severe. In his "Lightning-Rod Man" Melville had ridiculed the Reverend John Todd of Pittsfield for the ignorant terror he had (and continued to) spread, through his enormously "popular" *Students' Manual* (1835), on the ghastly consequences of male ONANISM.[19] In his *Conjugal Sins* Gardner wrote that

18. *Proceedings of the Massachusetts Historical Society* 87 (1975): 140.
19. See Chapter 4.

Todd's book had done "incalculable good in moulding the minds of American youth."[20] The doctor ascribed "lassitude and physical and mental feebleness" in "the modern [American] woman" to the same practice (*Conjugal Sins*, 70).

If the unstoppability of the miraculous machine in the papermill was "specially terrible" to Melville's narrator, Melville's once-upon-a-time friend Gardner was of the enemy. If onanism was a sin against God, other alternatives to pregnancy were worse. Gardner wrote for the right-to-life believers of his time when he printed what he doubtless preached on the matter of contraception. "Of the use of intermediate tegumentary coverings, made of thin rubber or gold-beater's skin . . . Madame de Stael is reputed to have said: 'They are cobwebs for protection, and bulwarks against love.' . . . Their employment certainly must produce a feeling of shame and disgust utterly destructive of the true delight of pure hearts. . . . They are suggestive of licentiousness and the brothel, and their employment degrades to bestiality the true feelings of manhood and the holy state of matrimony" (*Conjugal Sins*, 109).

Gardner was out to "Arrest the Rapid Extinction of the Native American People." Abortion in mid-century America has been called "epidemic," and (at least up to mid-term) was quite legal. His chapter on the subject is called "Infanticide." "Murder! Murder in cold blood" (*Conjugal Sins*, 111). The tactic was exactly Todd's: terrify already frightened women, as with the abortionist who failed the attempt, so that a child was born "shockingly mutilated, with one eye entirely put out and the brain so injured that . . ." (128). He reidentified the source of American woman's "present degeneracy" as "personal abuse" ("so utterly incurable," 220). He tried hard to discourage the use of the treadle sewing machine.[21]

Besides, contraception and abortion were both unnecessary. As early as 1856 Gardner had established his authority in his *Causes and Curative Treatment of Sterility* and its section on "The Physiology of Gestation," with the drawings and full-color pelvic interiors. The Conjugal solution was extremely simple: "conception cannot take

20. *Conjugal Sins* (New York: J. S. Redfield, 1870), 69.
21. *Lamb's Biographical Dictionary of the United States* (Boston: James H. Lamb Co., 1900), 223.

place, except during the first days following menstruation" (185). (He was expert on male sexuality as well: "the penis acquires, after [sic] its introduction into the vagina, a considerable volume . . . by reason of a bone which gives solidarity to it" [104]. "Curious information," as Howard said.) It is hard not to wonder if Melville followed the important female timetable as directed.

V

If "Tartarus" was not protesting indignities brought by the industrial revolution, what did Melville mean it to express? In an especially autobiographical section of *Pierre* (Book IX), he offered a clue. Among Pierre's books, the *Inferno* and *Hamlet* were "uppermost." "Dante," Melville says of Pierre, "had made him furious." He does not mean reading Dante. He means reading about Dante: what happened to him, according to Cary's prefatory thirty-two-page "Life of Dante" in his translation. "The man Dante Alighieri," Pierre tells himself, "received unforgivable affronts and insults from the world; and the poet Dante Alighieri bequeathed his immortal curse to it, in the sublime malediction of the Inferno."

Cary explains how Dante was persuaded on the death of Beatrice to marry Gemma Donati, by whom he had "numerous offspring." She was "a source of the bitterest suffering to him," writes Cary, citing the poet's own despair as expressed by a character in the *Inferno* (Canto XVI, 45–47):

> . . . whom, past doubt, my wife,
> Of savage temper, more than aught beside,
> Hath to this evil brought.

A heavy charge. Born and nurtured in Florence, Dante was for political reasons dispossessed, banished, and sentenced to death by burning. "Even to the ripeness of age," he wrote, "in exile and poverty," he wished "with all my heart, to rest this wearied spirit" and end his years a Florentine. "I have gone about like a mendicant

. . . a vessel without sail and without steerage." One day, he promised himself, he would stand at his "baptismal font" and "claim the wreath / Due to the poet's temples" (*Purgatory*, xxv). In 1321 he died at Ravenna. Somewhat later (162 years) a sepulchre was erected for him, and five centuries after his time a monument to him went up in Florence. Melville, infuriated, had no way of knowing how long or severe his own banishment would be.

Pierre is a curse on the world its hero rejects in suicide. For some, "Tartarus" is a curse on the enslavement of females to mills and factories. Readers who continue to believe this infer a social consciousness Melville never for a moment reveals in this story. The narrator fleetingly detects the Maids' "beseeching" image. But the only thing he feels for them is "some pained homage." Homage to what? To "their pale virginity."

> "All maids."
> Again the strange emotion filled me.

To their imprisonment the seedsman does not respond. He pities the fact they have never knc⁀ .. men. Such compassion would (will) not please everyone, but that does not alter the text.

Many will not be pleased either to accept the fact that it is the machine itself—its "unbudging fatality"—the narrator finds terrible. Epiphany unexpected: a revelation of the depth and passion of the author's frustration that anything more—pregnancy, children, family—should interfere with his doomed, Dantean determination to get by his pen recognition he had already earned. ("I and My Chimney," in its wry, oblique way, expresses the same unshakable resolution.) "Tartarus" is an unapologetic testament of fruitless anger at the "metallic necessity" that governs the reproduction of the species. To what end?

There is no help for it. Pierre explains how Shakespeare fits in: "Dante had made him fierce, and Hamlet insinuated that there was none to strike." That's how it was. Last seen on his journey home, the seedsman, all alone with inscrutable nature, is unarmed and aimless.

FATHERS AND SONS

8

"These Be Thy Gods, O Ahab!"

You explain nothing, O poet, but through you all things
become explainable.
                              —Paul Claudel, *La Ville* (1897)

There is no telling the quantities of energy by now expended on
Moby-Dick. Not without reason spent. The book offers—and a lot
more—"one of the most overwhelming myths ever invented on the
subject of man against evil" (Camus).[1] Thus it is not easy to explain
why there are no more than partial, contradictory, and often pitiful
attempts to cope with a crucial part of the novel: to sort out and
comprehend the transcendent beings Ahab summons, insults, or
appeals to in chapter 119, "The Candles." Toward the end of these
six pages arrives his top soliloquy, the story's spiritual climax. Here
he climbs to the peak of his cosmic defiance, boldness of thought and
language, and what F. O. Matthiessen called "staggering indiffer-
ence" to anything outside himself.[2] After this it is all downwind, the
final chase and wreck.

The speech is very often quoted, sometimes fully. But seldom if
ever explained. Ahab addresses, and mostly defies, the gods. What
gods? How many? On what grounds? Speaking to the "spirit of
lightning," what does he mean "thou leapest out of darkness; but I

1. Albert Camus, "Herman Melville," in *Lyrical and Critical Essays*, ed. Philip Thody (New
York: Alfred A. Knopf, 1969), 289.
2. F. O. Matthiessen, *American Renaissance: Art and Expression in the Age of Emerson
and Whitman* (New York: Oxford University Press, 1941), 430.

am darkness leaping out of light, leaping out of thee!" Three lines later, who and where is the "sweet mother" he calls for? How does he "glory" in his "genealogy" (which is unknown)? What could be God's "unparticipated grief"? "Beyond" God or the Creator, who or what does Ahab "dimly see"?

For some, such questions do not exist. Students of *Cliff's Notes* were recently told that Ahab is simply "addressing the sun." Paul Brodtkorb, Jr., says he talks to the corpusants, St. Elmo's fire (same thing), and the "fire gods."[3] No need to pile up reductions. It is obvious that Ahab has an awful lot on his mind.

In the new Northwestern-Newberry text of *Moby-Dick*,[4] Ahab declaims for thirty-seven lines (507–8), split into a pair of paragraphs by a stage direction. They go to the heart of him, hence of the work. They also go to the heart of Melville's "Quarrel with God," in Lawrance Thompson's phrase.[5] But though Thompson agrees that the "climactic action" of the whole novel lies in this chapter, he gives it a scant four pages (229–33), printing the outburst entire and explaining not a line of it. (He does have a good paragraph on Ahab's pride at the end.)

As dramatic as the rhetoric is the setting of this speech. A typhoon has hit the *Pequod* off Japan "like an exploding bomb upon a dazed and sleepy town." Toward evening the ship is torn of its canvas; in the dark, sky and sea still "roared and split with the thunder, and blazed with the lightning." After midnight new sails are reefed, and by morning the ship sails stunned: headed east, according to both its compasses, the sun is astern. The crew, sworn to hunt down the Whale, is in a "terror of dismay."

Readers who have paid real attention should be wondering what has hit them. The scene had been electrified by corposant flames that light the deck like giant tapers. Ahab begins addressing that fire.

3. *Ishmael's White World* (New Haven: Yale University Press, 1965), 71–75.

4. *The Writings of Herman Melville*, ed. Harrison Hayford, Hershel Parker, and G. Thomas Tanselle, 12 vols. to date (Evanston and Chicago: Northwestern University Press and The Newberry Library, 1968–), vol. 6, *Moby-Dick* (1988). Except where noted, references to other Melville works are to this edition: vol. 3, *Mardi* (1970); vol. 4, *Redburn* (1969); vol. 5, *White-Jacket* (1970); vol. 7, *Pierre* (1971); and vol. 9, *The Piazza Tales and Other Prose Pieces, 1839–1860* (1987).

5. *Melville's Quarrel with God* (Princeton: Princeton University Press, 1952).

But Melville's audience—for better than a half century not there—is soon in need of help. Melville, like Ishmael, has "swam through libraries." At this pitch of passion Ahab's mind is well armed; it strikes at will. It is the very mind Melville had announced two years earlier in *Mardi* (1849):

> Like a frigate, I am full with a thousand souls . . . running shouting across my decks. . . . Like a grand, ground swell, Homer's old organ rolls its vast volumes under the light frothy wave-crests . . . and high over my ocean, sweet Shakespeare soars. . . . I list to St. Paul. . . . Zeno murmurs maxims beneath the hoarse shout of Democritus . . . and Zoroaster whispered me before I was born. (367–68)

Since there has been no real exploration of this mind at its climax, best help lies in the notes to three editions of *Moby-Dick*: the Hendricks House 1952 edition by Luther S. Mansfield and Howard Vincent; the Bobbs-Merrill 1964 version by Charles Feidelson, Jr., and Harold Beaver's erratic Penguin entry in 1972. (The notes for first and last are book length in themselves; there are useful notes in other editions, but not to "The Candles.") Put together, however, there are still questions, deep differences, doubts. (Feidelson and Beaver are best.)

Elsewhere, understanding of Ahab's deities is neither plentiful nor usually helpful. In *The Wake of the Gods* Bruce Franklin has a relevant notion: that the typhoon itself represents a supernatural being— Typhon, Greek monster or giant. "Melville uses the uncapitalized word "typhoon" . . . several times early in *Moby-Dick*," he says, "and later capitalized it to evoke the mythic being"; it is "also addressed as a god by Ahab."[6] Interesting, if accurate. But typhoon in lower case appears only once (90), and is never addressed at all by Ahab— who, in chapter 116, "The Dying Whale," appeals to a strange "dark Hindoo half of nature" *in* the Typhoon (497). Beaver somehow accepts Franklin's reading. And Typhon may well have been on Melville's mind (he has been called "father of the winds") when he

6. (Stanford: Stanford University Press, 1963), 78–80.

used the capital, but he did nothing with the association save provide an overtone. (Tony Tanner would not agree. In a new introduction to *Moby-Dick*, he says that the whale is Typhon, hunted by the priest-king-god Osiris.[7] This supreme "Ur-myth" is behind the whole book, he argues unpersuasively.)

The first god clearly summoned in the storm carries no weight either. As thunder rolls overhead someone (Stubb?) asks, "Who's there?" Ahab says, "Old Thunder!" Unremarked irony may be the point; as a novice Ishmael had asked "Who's Old Thunder?" and had been told "Captain Ahab," some called him that. But Thor is the obvious reference.

First sign of the God of the Old Testament appears with the corposants (Melville's corpusants). He calls them "God's burning finger . . . laid upon the ship," weaving "Mene, Mene, Tekel, Upharsin" into the *Pequod*'s doomed shrouds and cordage. Each of the three tall masts was "silently burning in the sulphurous air, like three gigantic wax tapers before an altar" (505). Churchly expectations are averted. Fedallah the Parsee, member of a Zoroastrian sect associated with fire, is kneeling before Ahab, who puts his foot on him and cries

> Oh! thou clear spirit of clear fire, whom on these seas I as Persian once did worship, till in the sacramental act so burned by thee, that to this hour I bear the scar. . . . I now know that thy right worship is defiance. To neither love nor reverence wilt thou be kind; and e'en for hate thou canst but kill; and all are killed. No fearless fool now fronts thee.

All right so far. Once a Zoroastrian, Ahab worshipped his god's manifestation in fire as destructive of evil until he was badly burned—by lightning, perhaps. Thus it may be that good and evil are not separate but one.[8] He does not speak to Zoroaster, Persian prophet, or Mazda the deity, but to the sign of him. (Votaries do not, as

---

7. (New York: Oxford University Press, 1988), xxvi–xxvii.
8. See Charles Walcutt, "The Fire Symbolism in *Moby-Dick*," *Modern Language Notes* 4 (May 1944): 304–10.

believed, worship fire, but consider it emblematic of the god.) Ahab
worshipped not fire but its "spirit."

The paragraph that begins with fire does not stick to its subject.
Ahab's charged brain changes target without notice, one god apparently triggering others. Next appears to be the Christian God in both
Old and New Testament forms, as befits Ahab's background. (He was
one of those Nantucket "Quakers with a vengeance"—a reminder
that "thee, thou, thy" and the rest are not archaic or poetic in him
but natural.) Without a break he says

> I own thy speechless, placeless power; but to the last gasp of
> my earthquake life will dispute its unconditional, unintegral
> mastery in me. In the midst of the personified impersonal, a
> personality stands here. Though but a point at best; whence-
> soe'er I came; wheresoe'er I go; yet while I earthly live, the
> queenly personality lives in me, and feels her royal rights.
> . . . Come in thy lowest form of love, and I will kneel and kiss
> thee; but at thy highest, come as mere supernal power; and
> though thou launchest navies of full-freighted worlds, there's
> that in here that still remains indifferent.

This is as assertive as even Ahab can get, and can be approached
only in parts. Starting at the bottom, the launcher of worlds sounds
like the God of Genesis that floated this one. In the lowest (most
human) form of love, he would be Jesus. But the main point is Ahab's
utmost refusal to concede this power in its "highest" absolute
dominion over him, or even to admit his own inferiority. He knows
that he is a person, with a real—even sovereign, he declares—
personality. For Ahab (as Feidelson suggests) God is only a personi-
fication of forces themselves personless. A name, a title, an abstrac-
tion, not a person like a father. He will not grant this force complete
control over him, or acknowledge fealty. Then, having left the spirit
of fire far behind, abruptly he returns to it—now enigmatically calling
it father: " 'Oh, thou clear spirit, of thy fire thou madest me, and like
a true child of fire, I breathe it back to thee.' " (Flashes of lightning
and leaping flames.) Still to the lightning Ahab says

> Thou canst blind; but I can then grope. Thou canst consume;
> but I can then be ashes. . . . The lightning flashes through
> my skull . . . my whole beaten brain seems as beheaded, and
> rolling on some stunning ground. Oh, oh! Yet . . . will I talk
> to thee. Light though thou be, thou leapest out of darkness;
> but I am darkness leaping out of light, leaping out of thee!
> . . . Oh, thou magnanimous! now I do glory in my genealogy.
> But thou art but my fiery father; my sweet mother, I know
> not. Oh, cruel! What hast thou done with her?

Ahab's own crazy mother is long dead, as he knows. How lightning
could be his father is not yet explainable—or why he has such pride
in his ancestry, which but for his parents is never mentioned. Melville
is trailing the genealogies of "high mortal miseries . . . among the
sourceless primogenitures" (464) of the gods—not all identified. At
once he returns to the Old Testament God of Christians. Now he
assaults. The whereabouts of his sweet mother is his "puzzle," he
admits. "But thine is greater": "Thou knowest not how came ye,
hence callest thyself unbegotten; certainly knowest not thy beginning, hence callest thyself unbegun. I know that of me, which thou
knowest not of thyself, oh, thou omnipotent."

Having derided, Ahab is encouraged to demote the Creator, and
does: "There is some unsuffusing thing beyond thee . . . to whom
all thy eternity is but time, all thy creativeness mechanical." Feidelson explains this succinctly and reasonably. Ahab reflects the Gnostic
belief in the Demiurge, the creative god of matter who made this
world, as opposed to the remote and "truly Divine Being" (the
unsuffusing thing "beyond thee," which is Spirit). The concept comes
from Plato, Gnosticism being a late Hellenistic–early Christian heresy
which Melville clearly knew of. (He mentioned Gnostics back in
White-Jacket [1850], where the *Man-of-War*'s chaplain was "particularly hard" on them [156].) In the chapter "Moby Dick," moreover,
he makes knowing reference to the Ophites, a Gnostic sect that also
believed in an inferior god of matter, hostile to spirituality, and
worshipped most heretically the serpent of Eden, for trying to give
Adam and Eve knowledge withheld from them by Jehovah.

There is another side to this knowledge of parentage that Ahab possesses and God lacks. Melville is full of orphans and by-blows. He felt himself an orphan; "our souls," he writes in *Moby-Dick*, are like orphans. Ishmael seems one long before in the last word of the book he so calls himself. Pip is a cast-off; Ahab was orphaned beyond question, his father having died before he was born and his mother when he was twelve months. (His son will soon be fatherless.) But the worst sort of orphan is the foundling, deserted by parents unknown. Ahab saves this disaster for God, calling him a "foundling fire." This is his "incommunicable riddle," his "unparticipated grief" that none lament. On top of this he lays a final insult: "hermit immemorial," that hides himself since history began. About to have his attack terminated by a typhonic freak, Ahab ends it with lightning and fatherhood: "Here again with haughty agony, I read my sire. . . . I leap with thee; . . . would fain be welded with thee, defyingly I worship thee!"

> "The boat! The boat!" cried Starbuck, "look at thy boat, old man!"
>
> Ahab's harpoon . . . remained firmly lashed in its conspicuous crotch, so that it projected beyond his whale-boat's bow; but the sea that had stove its bottom had caused the loose leather sheath to drop off; and from the keen steel barb there now came a levelled flame of pale, forked fire . . . like a serpent's tongue . . . and snatching the burning harpoon. Ahab waved it like a torch among them.

A moment for Freudians or Ophites (Ophite sects were known for extreme license) quickly passes. "Look ye here," Ahabs commands; "thus I blow out the last fear!" And with one breath he extinguishes the flame.

According to some, Thomas Vargish in particular,[9] more Gnosticism is needed to understand "The Candles." Supreme for Gnostics is "spiritual essence," and the source of spirit in man is the goddess Sophia, "wisdom." Out of overweening love for the Supreme Being she conceived the Demiurge—creator of the material world, which

9. See Thomas Vargish, "Gnostic Mythos in *Moby-Dick*," *PMLA* 81 (June 1966): 272–77.

world is inherently evil. She was both his mother and foe. Melville
would have known her from Andrews Norton's *The Evidences of the
Genuineness of the Gospels*[10] (which, as Lawrance Thompson observes [430], he "could hardly have escaped knowing," so widely
was it read, reviewed, quoted). It is virtually "certain," Vargish
argues, "that Melville freely adopted the Gnostic mythos . . .
especially as it treated the 'primogenitures of the gods' . . . and the
virtue of Sophia, the 'sweet mother' " (277).

But Ahab in "The Dying Whale," a few pages before "The Candles," had appealed to a very different, nameless "queen." "Oh," he
calls on a wondrous, placid evening (497), "thou dark Hindoo half of
nature, who of drowned bones hast builded thy separate throne
somewhere in the heart of these unverdured seas . . . infidel . . .
queen. . . . [R]ock me with a prouder if a darker faith. All thy
unnameable imminglings float beneath me here." Associating this
magic, nameless figure with Sophia clarifies nothing. But without
much explanation Vargish claims that *this* "queen" represents the
"female principle" to Ahab, and is his "sweet mother," the Indian
analogue of the Gnostic Sophia (275). The connection between such
unlike theologies, he explains, is "the strange conception . . . of
assigning a spouse to the Supreme Being." (Not exactly, in Hindu-
ism, to him alone!)

Feidelson does not mention Sophia. Beaver does not identify
Ahab's mother, but he flatly states that the Hindu goddess is "Kali,
Siva's consort, black goddess of death, with her necklace of human
heads and protruding blood-stained tongue." As traditionally represented, however, Kali is not "dark" but jet- or blue-black. She is
hideous as can be. Why should Ahab want her to rock him in a
"prouder, if a darker faith"? Where is evidence that Melville ever
heard of Kali? It is true that Andrews Norton also saw a connection
between Gnostic and Hindu theology, but it consists in "remarkable
coincidences," and coincidence by definition is accidental. Like Sophia, Hindu goddesses are "subordinate powers of their respective
lords"—so runs the argument—and both represent the "female
principle."

10. 3 vols. (Boston: J. B. Russell, 1837–44), 3:119.

This merger of supernatural powers who gave mythic birth to Ahab is surely unsatisfactory. And none of it gives him pause. The pressing question is whence came the pride that breathes fire in the face of a god—that indeed allows Melville to call him a god: "God help thee, old man, thy thoughts have created a creature in thee; and he whose intense thinking thus makes him a Prometheus: a vulture feeds upon that heart forever" (202), as on the Greek god's liver. The answer shortly preceded *Moby-Dick*, for the book was not quite finished when Melville tipped his thinking to Hawthorne in a well known letter (mid-April 1851). He had been pondering "the tragicalness of human thought in its own unbiased native, and profounder workings." He was struck with

> the apprehension of the absolute condition of present things as they strike the eye of the man who fears them not, though they do their worst to him,—the man who . . . declares himself a sovereign nature (in himself) amid the powers of heaven, hell, and earth. He may perish; but so long as he exists he insists upon treating with all Powers upon an equal basis.[11]

(Ahab to Starbuck: "Talk not to me of blasphemy, man; I'd strike the sun if it insulted me. . . . Who's over me? Truth hath no confines." Starbuck, murmuring, "God keep me!—keep us all!" [164].)

How Ahab came by that pride might once have seemed the secret of *Moby-Dick*, but the answer has been around quite a while. Working at a pitch of imaginative energy unprecedented on these shores, Melville had driven Ahab to the full stature of tragic heroism—and

11. *The Letters of Herman Melville*, ed. Merrell R. Davis and William H. Gilman (New Haven: Yale University Press, 1960), 124–25. A direct and significant (but apparently unremarked) Melvillean echo of Emerson is audible here. Ahab's "queenly personality" with its "royal rights," and the "mind who declares himself a sovereign nature (in himself)," were anticipated in 1842 by "The Transcendentalist," where Emerson resorts for his own argument to the German philosopher, Friedrich Heinrich Jacobi (1743–1819), who invokes man's "sovereign right," conferred by "the majesty of his being," to determine right and wrong with his "private spirit," as Ahab does (*The Collected Works of Ralph Waldo Emerson*, ed. Alfred R. Ferguson and Joseph Slater et al., 4 vols. to date [Cambridge: Harvard University Press, 1971–], vol. 1, *Nature, Addresses, and Lectures* [1971], ed. Ferguson, p. 205).

charged him with an eloquence that rings across a ravaged deck. Stanley T. Geist, a Harvard undergraduate, appears to have been first to spell this out, in 1939, with publication of his honors thesis, *Herman Melville: The Tragic Vision and the Heroic Ideal.*[12] "Grief and Greatness, suffering and heroism," he writes; "these were, to Melville, inseparable" (as to *King Lear*) (44). He puts it more clearly than did Melville to Hawthorne, focusing on

> Melville's firm conviction that man became a hero of gigantic stature by attaining the vision of tragedy. . . . [T]hat he was himself among the giants, made his use of the Promethean symbol particularly appropriate. For if the greatness of the individual, residing wholly within his own vision of the world, was contingent upon no one and nothing outside himself, what distinction remained on the timeless and bodiless spiritual plane between human and superhuman? . . . What more could the gods themselves know of the depths of human tragedy than the profoundest men? If no more, why should the hero abase himself before any powers, human or superhuman? (48)

Grief and suffering: the indelible marks of Ahab when, after twenty-seven chapters he first appeared to the narrator (123–24). Where is the literary character more powerfully introduced? "Reality outran apprehension," says Ishmael. "Captain Ahab stood upon his quarter-deck . . . like a man cut away from the stake." A slender "rod-like mark, lividly whitish," ran down his face into his clothing, branding him like a lightning-struck great tree. (Some thought him birthmarked "from crown to sole.") Not a word to his officers: "moody stricken Ahab" stood before his crew "with a crucifixion in his face." Partly stood—on a "barbaric white leg" made of whale-jaw. ("Aye, he was mismasted off Japan. . . . He has a quiver of 'em.") (123–24).

He also has (Geist again) what it takes to flesh out the tragic hero: Promethean defiance of the gods and concentrated pride. Driving his mind into the depths called for self-reliance that faced a cheerless fate. "[T]he gods themselves are not forever glad," Ahab reminds

12. (Cambridge: Harvard University Press, 1939).

himself. "The ineffaceable sad birthmark in the brow of man, is but the stamp of sorrow in the signers" (464). If not for rank and isolation, Ahab would have found a soulmate in Ishmael, despite temperaments. It is Ishmael who thinks "The truest of all men was the Man of Sorrows, and the truest of all books is Solomon's, and Ecclesiastes is the fine hammered steel of woe. 'All is vanity.' ALL" (424).

But the prouder if darker faith? The triumph of Ahab's convictions comes, paradoxically, as he is killed and Ishmael saved. When he sees that he and the 'god-bullied hull" of his ship are going down separately (he tied to the "damned whale," sounding), he achieves apotheosis: "lonely death on lonely life! Oh, now I feel my topmost greatness lies in my topmost grief." Suffering, grief, and the stature of tragic heroism are one at the moment of extinction. What has silenced most commentary—darkness emerging from light as equal—is clearer. Illumination born of thought led Ahab to the dark knowledge of tragedy, as powerful as its source.

It was the lightning, his "fiery father," that Ahab asked of his sweet mother, "what hast thou done with her?" The primogeniture of his gods lies in still another myth, other gods, hitherto unnoticed. Melville had them from Euripides, having bought three volumes of his work on March 19, 1849.[13] All he needed was the first drama, "The Bacchae," which begins:

> I come,
> Bacchus, the son of Jove, whom Semele,
> Daughter of Cadmus, mid the lightning flames
> Brought forth. . . .

13. Translated by the Reverend R. Potter; see Merton M. Sealts, Jr., *Melville's Reading*, rev. and enl. ed. (Columbia: University of South Carolina Press, 1988), 167. Melville knew something of Semele, however, by the time he was nineteen. In the second of his two "Fragments from a Writing Desk," which appeared in the *Democratic Press and Lansingburgh Advertiser* for May 18, 1839, he mentions "several magnificent pictures illustrative of the loves of Jupiter and Semele" and others (see *The Piazza Tales*, 202). Nor did he forget her in 1876. Near the end of *Clarel*, Don Hannibal says "Among reformers in true way / There's one—the imp of Semele; / Ay, and brave Raleigh too, we'll say. / Wine and the weed! blest innovations!" (see *Clarel: A Poem and Pilgrimage in the Holy Land*, in *The Writings of Herman Melville*, ed. Harrison Hayford, Alma A. MacDougall, Hershel Parker, and G. Thomas Tanselle, Historical and Critical Note by Walter Bezanson (Evanston and Chicago: Northwestern University Press and The Newberry Library, 1991), 12:451–52.

The myth, sometimes called "The Birth of Dionysus," tells how
Semele was loved by Jove. Juno found out and as usual was vengeful.
In disguise she appeared to Semele and persuaded her to ask her
lover to prove his identity by coming to her in his divinity's full
magnificence. Jove, most unwilling, was tricked into compliance; in
his splendor and the fire of his lightning Semele was destroyed. But
Jove plucked her unborn child from the ruins of its mother, and
sewed him into his thigh, from which Bacchus was born in due
course. With Ahab's comment " 'Oh, thou magnanimous! now I do
glory in my genealogy. But . . . my sweet mother, I know not. Oh,
cruel! what hast thou done with her?' " another soul has run across
his deck. Again he is himself a god—with, it may be, a head-to-toe
birthmark to show for it. Once again, "Our souls are like those
orphans whose unwedded mothers die in bearing them" (492).

But, as Ahab says, "a little lower layer." Matthiessen, in his still
valuable if embattled *American Renaissance* (430), paused over "Oh,
thou clear spirit, of thy fire thou madest me," and planted a seed
that seems never to have sprouted. What he wrote was "it is by no
means clear exactly how much Melville meant to imply in making
Ahab regard the fire as his father"—and presently to repeat it, "my
fiery father." Though never asserted, it is likely that Melville meant
to imply a good deal. In all the holy fire, what is hardest to measure
is how far his Quarrel with God was an unextinguished quarrel with
Allan Melville ("Here . . . I read my sire"). The tortured, passionate
psyche that created Ahab had more cause than was known in
Matthiessen's day for desecrating the memory of his father, the fiery
"spirit" that made Herman. *Redburn*, partly autobiographical, made
plain what a wound the boy suffered at twelve when the "marvelous
being" Redburn had thought his father went into delirium and died,[14]
leaving nothing behind but debt (crooked bankruptcy at that). It was
the end of the family; Redburn "almost strangles" to recall. Michael
Paul Rogin puts the financial side of it plainly: *The Confidence Man*,
bitterest of his books, "is Melville's novel about his father."[15] Then

14. A whole book has been made of that death and the son; see Neal L. Tolchin, *Mourning,
Gender, and Creativity in the Art of Herman Melville* (New Haven: Yale University Press, 1988).
The author says that Ahab's speech in "The Candles" reflects Melville's father's "deathbed
mania" (118–19). (It was printed entire in Louis Untermeyer's *American Poetry from the
Beginning to Whitman* [New York: Harcourt, Brace, 1931], 560–61.)

15. *Subversive Genealogy: The Politics and Art of Herman Melville* (Berkeley and Los
Angeles: University of California Press, 1985), 249–53.

at nineteen Herman learned, like Pierre in *Pierre*, that Allan had fathered a daughter he never confessed. (At once Pierre felt "driven out an infant Ishmael into the desert with no maternal Hagar" [89].)

The resentment "beyond" or beneath or behind the attack on gods in "The Candles" had its ultimate source in Melville Senior. In 1925 the late Dr. Henry A. Murray gave Sigmund Freud a copy of *Moby-Dick*. Predictably Freud pronounced the Whale a "father figure."[16] For the book as a whole, very well. But in "The Candles," where Ahab summons gods in his soliloquy, he does not think of his watery enemy. At this crucial point the ultimate father figure is Herman Melville's father. How like a god!—pious, self-righteous, sententious, judgmental, sincere, he was the first god a boy had known and the first he would outgrow.

But childhood wounds never heal. "Talk not of the bitterness of middle-age and after life," warns Redburn. "A boy can feel all that, and much more. . . . And never again can such blights be made good; they strike in too deep, and leave such a scar that the air of Paradise might not erase it" (11). First to put it bluntly was Lewis Mumford in 1929: "Both Melville's father and mother were monsters."[17] Call him Ishmael, driven out by Abraham with no maternal Hagar. A boy who felt rejected by his father suffers permanently. By his overbearing mother as well, differently but permanently (especially when long living in the same house). In old age Melville still felt it: "she hated me," he told his niece.[18] Any account of his boyhood that touches on his childhood will show Herman overmatched in a struggle for his parents' esteem and affection by a brilliant, handsome older brother Gansevoort. Herman idolized his father; when he was seven Allan reported to his brother-in-law that the boy "is very backward in speech & somewhat slow in comprehension, but . . . of a docile & amiable disposition."[19] (In *Pierre*, Pierre, stabbing himself, thinks "docile" eleven times in less than a page [19–20].) Gansevoort, according to his father, was "rather more than a genius." (Rather

---

16. *New York Times*, June 24, 1988, D17 (Murray's obituary).

17. But "they were correct and meritorious members of society, and it is difficult to believe that the image of God can err, if it be repeated often enough" (Lewis Mumford, *Herman Melville* [New York: Harcourt, Brace, 1929], 15).

18. See Newton Arvin, *Herman Melville* (New York: William Sloane, 1950), 30.

19. See, for example, Edwin Haviland Miller's *Melville* (New York: George Braziller, 1975), 64–71.

more like his father he broke down at thirty and died in a month.) Melville waited until his sixth book to get to "The Candles," and he needed two more to discharge it all, but anger will out—though ambivalence remain (as in "my sire . . . defyingly I worship thee!").

What Matthiessen did not remark is how Ahab emphasized the "spirit" of fire ("clear spirit, of thy fire thou madest me"). It does not seem to have occurred to him that Melville might have stressed the word in hope that some would read him to mean what Shakespeare meant when he described "lust in action" as "the expense of spirit in a waste of shame" (Sonnet 129). Melville knew a Hawthorne story, "The Artist of the Beautiful" (1844), in which "expend" and "spirit" are used repeatedly in this sense. In the midst of Ahab's rhetorical ejaculations, that sprinkle the text with exclamation points, and of leaping, burning fires, plus an unsheathed harpoon spitting flame like a snake's tongue, the suggestion of Priapus, a "fringe god" related to phallic cults like the Dionysian, is urgent.

No part of Ahab's layered speech, but the reason for the whole novel, is the first and last god in it—a mythic being exalted above nature by a crazy captain/tragic hero. Visibly a god from the reader's first closeup: "Not the white bull Jupiter swimming away with ravished Europa clinging to his graceful horns . . . not Jove, not that great majesty Supreme! did surpass the glorified White Whale as he so divinely swam" (548). As he slowly rose, "his whole marbleized body formed a high arch . . . and warningly waving his bannered flukes in the air, the grand god revealed himself, sounded, and went out of sight" (549).

Melville had been apprehensive of "present things" cultural in America. Rightly so. If on publication *Moby-Dick* formed a bannered arch before it sounded, few watched. This blindness, Newton Arvin wrote soberly, is "the heaviest count in our literary annals against the American mind."[20] (Among illiterates the book still has a reputation for dullness.) No great surprise to Melville, who foresaw the fate of his work and slaved to finish it anyhow. For Hawthorne (early June 1851) he predicted his future: "My dear Sir, a presentiment is on me,—I shall at last be worn out and perish, like an old nutmeg

---

20. Arvin, *Herman Melville*, 202.

grater. . . . What I feel most moved to write, that is banned,—it will not pay. . . . Though I wrote the Gospels in this century. I should die in the gutter."[21] Four decades later he died in a gutter—in a private, final flicker of a low flame. In a sense he had written Gospel: Old English *godspell*, modern English "good news." Good news that a half-crippled captain of a worn whaler could make an affirmation of self, of irreducible personality, more powerful than any asserted by Whitman or Emerson or Thoreau, Melville's formidable native competition. Good news that he could stand Ahab face to face in defiance of gods. (In America, he could have done it *only* in his century.) The tragic hero of *Moby-Dick* is mad; in driving a shipload of hapless sailors to their deaths he is criminal; in his pride he veers all out of bounds.

But he is Ahab, the "mighty pageant creature, formed for noble tragedy"—a vision early in the book (37) come alive. He overrides objection. Melville was banking on it—on "poetic faith," the eager suspension of disbelief he now enjoys. His hero is the peglegged veteran of awesome seaborne struggles. Furious and fearless to death, he stabs with his own harpoon the leviathan all would have him flee, which at once sinks him and his crew and soon every chip of his vessel.

Everyone knows that Ahab. Fewer know the extravagant cosmologist, conversant with large religions and forgotten heresy, along with more than a dozen gods, goddesses, and mythic beings—not all, very likely, as yet revealed. To the soul of this Ahab, the wild paragraphs lit by corposants are both the royal road and shortest cut.

---

21. *Letters*, 128–29.

9

The Last Good-Bye: "Daniel Orme"

Your old tars are all Daniels.
—*Mardi* (1849)

Ormer is a contraction of *Oreille de Mer*. [The fish] clingeth
to the Rock with the Back, and the Shell covers the Belly.
—Michael Donovan,
Domestic Economy (1830)

The story survives in Herman Melville's hand. Thirty-three years
after he died in New York, "Daniel Orme" was published in London.
It had been found in Wellesley Farms, Massachusetts, in 1919, the
centenary of the author's birth, by Raymond Weaver. There it rested
in a folder along with *Billy Budd*, unfinished, in a box of manuscripts
recently given the writer's first grandchild, Eleanor Melville Metcalf,
by her mother. It is the last piece of writing Melville lived to
complete. Weaver added a mistaken parenthesis to the title (omitted
from *Billy Budd*), and without comment published the tale in his
edition of volume 13 of Melville's *Works* (London: Constable, 1924).[1]

Chief responsibility for its neglect belongs to academics. A new
Reader's Guide to the Short Stories of Herman Melville provides a
substantial "compendium of historical and critical data for each of
Melville's sixteen short stories,"[2] the tour having bypassed "Orme."

1. "Daniel Orme," *The Works of Herman Melville*, vol. 13 (New York: Russell & Russell,
1963), 117–22.
2. *A Reader's Guide to the Short Stories of Herman Melville*, ed. Lea Bertani Vozar Newman
(Boston: G. K. Hall, 1986), ix.

Twice as big, there is now a *Companion to Melville Studies,* which appears to ignore nothing but it.[3] Since others may be unfamiliar with the text, here is a short account.

Meeting with an uncommunicative old sailor in his last refuge, Melville likens to coming across a meteoric stone in a field: "There it lies. . . . In what imaginable sphere did it get that strange, igneous look?" (117). The sailor got it from a cartridge explosion that "peppered all below the eyes with dense dottings of black blue" (118), not the first such accident in Melville. This was an old man-of-war's man whom the author calls Daniel Orme, quickly adding that "a sailor's name as it appears on a crew's list is not always his real name" (117). Turned seventy, Orme has slipped into moorings ashore, an undescribed home for retired seamen. He is moody, unsociable, and given to muttering. Sometimes he would "start, and with a look or gesture so uncheerfully peculiar that the Calvinist imagination of a certain frigate's chaplain construed it into remorseful condemnation of some dark deed in the past" (118).

He is striking in appearance, too. Large, strong features cast as in iron, he is "bowed somewhat in the shoulders . . . hands heavy and hard; short nails like withered horn. A powerful head, and shaggy. An iron-gray beard broad as a commodore's pennant" (119). He was a Great Grizzly awaiting the last hour, grim in his den. But he had a peculiar habit. When thinking himself alone he rolled aside the bosom of his Guernsey frock and steadfastly contemplated something on his body. Curious fellows drugged his tea at supper. Next morning an old-clothes man reported what he found:

> A crucifix in indigo and vermillion tattooed on the chest and on the side of the heart. Slanting across the crucifix and paling the pigment there ran a whitish scar . . . such as might ensue from the slash of a cutlass. (120)

Gossips told the landlady that Orme was "a sort of *man forbid*" (120), but she ignored them and he stayed on. His looks said *hands off.* Yet, let alone, he began to mellow into a sort of "animal decay"

3. *A Companion to Melville Studies,* ed. John Bryant (New York: Greenwood Press, 1986).

(121) that, Melville says, hazes the memory, softens the heart, and perhaps lulls the conscience.

On a fine Easter day he was discovered alone and dead "on a height overlooking the seaward sweep of the great haven to whose shore . . . he had moored" (121). It was a terrace built for war, neglected in peace, a sanctuary in solitude. An "obsolete battery of rusty guns" (121) was mounted there; he lay with his back to one of them, legs stretched before, clay pipe broken in half, bowl empty. Facing the outlet to the ocean the eyes were open, "continuing in death the vital glance fixed on the hazy waters and the dim-seen sails coming and going or at anchor nearby" (122).

About his last thoughts? the author continues. If there was anything to the stories about him, had remorse any part in these thoughts. Or did his "freaks, starts, eccentric shrugs and grimaces" point to nothing? And if there really was "something dark that he chose to keep to himself, what then? Such reticence may sometimes be more for the sake of others than one's self. No, let us believe that . . . he fell asleep recalling through the haze of memory many a far-off scene of the wide world's beauty dreamily suggested by the hazy waters before him" (122). He is buried among other sailors in a lonely plot overgrown with wild eglantine, sweetbriar, a rose with fragrant leaves and pink flowers.

Thus Melville dreamed of being dismissed in peace. "Daniel Orme" is a heartening, unsentimental tale, a profoundly resigned, quirky, but graceful and unembittered exit. More, Orme in his haven is remarkably like *Oedipus at Colonus*, his refuge a sacred grove outside Athens where he has come to die. Both strangers are at first unwelcome: Orme as "a sort of *man forbid* . . . branded by the Evil Spirit" (120), blind Oedipus regarded by a Greek chorus as a "wretched exile" ("dreadful his voice . . . terrible his aspect") and told "Away! Be gone!" Both remain, and in the end the chorus speaks for both in wishing them death in "easy steps." Melville and Sophocles wrote as old men with time running out, recounting the last days and passing of close-held characters in simple stories, postludes to stormy lives. Each left his work behind, unpublished, unperformed.[4]

4. Translation from the Greek here is by Thomas Francklin, whom Melville presumably read in the Harper & Brothers 1834 edition of Sophocles, which he owned. See Merton M.

More's the pity that the sailor's tale is so little known today, if known at all. Perhaps chance sightings have failed to recognize Melville behind Orme's beard, to which Melville's was identical. No doubt some cannot picture the writer (who turned seventy in 1889) as such an obscure and isolated figure by the sea when he died in New York of his heart's ailments in a small black iron bed on a rugless floor in a house on East 26th Street, where he lived for thirty years scarce known to the nearest neighbor. On September 29, 1891, the day after his death, the *New-York Daily Tribune* ran an obituary that said:

> He won considerable fame as an author by the publication of a book in 1847 entitled "Typee." . . . This was his best work, although he has since written a number of other stories, which were published more for private than public circulation.[5]

For a long time, "Orme" circulated not at all. Buried in the original sixteen-volume edition of Melville's works—reprinted in 1963 but still not to be found in a great many libraries—it gets around very little. There is no extended or critical study of the tale; the only "appreciation" of it one is likely to encounter is but a reference in Newton Arvin's 1950 biography of Melville, where the writer's last years are presented in terms of the story, those years having had for him

> the quality of a broadly tranquilizing exodus to a drama. . . . There is something extraordinarily suitable and satisfying to the imagination in the picture they present of touchily guarded solitude and rather grim obscurity. . . . There is something a little uncanny about him, to tell the truth, as there is about the old seaman Daniel Orme.[6]

Sealts, Jr., *Melville's Reading* (Madison: University of Wisconsin Press, 1966), 51. He probably read as well the four-page biographical sketch of the playwright that opens the book. If so, he learned that Sophocles had been accused of insanity and offered *Oedipus at Colonus* in his defense.

5. Jay Leyda, *The Melville Log*, 2 vols. (New York: Harcourt, Brace, 1951), 2:837.

6. Newton Arvin, *Herman Melville* (New York: William Sloane, 1950), 287–88.

Other scholars, who have looked at the story and responded, have seen little beyond the scarred tattoo. In *The Melville Archetype*, for instance, Martin Leonard Pops is much taken with that image, reducing it to chaos.[7] First he reports that Orme's chest bears scars of "crossed swords which form a crucifix."[8] Then he turns at length (157–67) to Melville's *Israel Potter* (1855), whose hero does have crossed-sword scars on his chest, neither of which Mr. Pops observes. Then, having completely forgotten his own description of Orme's distinguishing marks, he quotes Melville's. No turning back, he advances to the sailor's last sight of the world's beauty and explains that "even as Man nears death, he becomes aware of eternal life."[9]

Things got off on the wrong foot before Pops, and have never righted. In *Melville's Religious Thought* (1943), William Braswell concluded that Orme was Melville's "symbolic self-portrait," basing his insight on a grievous reading of the title, "Daniel, or me?"[10] He also submits that into the "beloved" and marred tattoo is "compressed the most moving part of [Melville's] own religious history."[11] Within a year his pun on "Orme" was sanctioned in *American Literature* by F. Barron Freeman.[12] But Freeman was preoccupied with his insistence that the whole point of the tale was its unquestionable relation to *Billy Budd*, which lies mostly in the Dansker, also grizzled with gunshot. (The "Daniel Orme" relation to *Billy Budd* is beyond dispute because Freeman so misread what Melville wrote on its folder—following Weaver in the Constable edition—that he thought "Orme" a leftover from the novel.)[13]

James Baird, not otherwise interested in "Daniel Orme," is princi-

7. Martin Leonard Pops, *The Melville Archetype* (Kent, Ohio: Kent State University Press, 1970).

8. Ibid., 21.

9. Ibid., 234.

10. William Braswell, *Melville's Religious Thought* (Durham: Duke University Press, 1943), 124.

11. Ibid., 125.

12. Barron Freeman, "The Enigma of Melville's 'Daniel Orme,' " *American Literature* 16 (1944): 208–11.

13. This mistake is explained by Harrison Hayford and Merton M. Sealts, Jr., editors of *Billy Budd, Sailor* (Chicago: University of Chicago Press, 1962), in their "History of the Text," 17–18.

pal interpreter of tattoos and scars.[14] It was in *Mardi*, Melville's third book, that he introduced the tattoo; it adorns Jarl, old seaman from Skye and companion to Taji, the protagonist. On his arm is "our Saviour on the cross, in blue; with the crown of thorns, and three drops of blood in vermillion, falling one by one from each hand and foot."[15] Jarl is vastly proud of his art work; Yillah, a mythic maiden aboard, is fascinated; neither Taji nor Melville offers any comment. Therefore Baird's response is of interest: "In Jarl's tattooing Melville reaches his first expression of feeling invoked *[sic]* by the image of the Christian cross, or the crucifixion, represented through a primitive art."[16] Moving to Orme's chest he explains that the scar slashed the promise of Redemption with "the forces of violence and evil."[17] Baird soon achieves an eloquence beyond intelligibility:

> God is here, in every element of this symbol: in its reference to primitive man, in its figure of the Man on the Cross, crucified by the emblem of war and violence, as though to negate, with an imperious divinity, the total meaning of human innocence. This scar is the brand of God, the same brand which Ahab has felt. . . . God brands all. So Melville seems to say in the symbol of a cross . . . on the body of Israel Potter . . . [who] wanders with the token of divine incomprehensibility carved into his flesh.[18]

Before "Daniel Orme," Melville had described a tattoo in relation to religious development of a sort. It belongs to Agath, "ocean's wrinkled son," who turns up in the poem *Clarel*. Encountered in the Holy Land, he is a "living fresco": "Upon the fore-arm did appear / A thing of art, vermil and blue, / A crucifixion in tattoo, / With trickling blood-drops strange to see."[19] He bears a Jerusalem cross as well.

---

14. James Baird, *Ishmael: A Study of the Symbolic Mode in Primitivism* (Baltimore: Johns Hopkins Press, 1956).

15. Herman Melville, *Mardi: and A Voyage Thither* (Evanston and Chicago: Northwestern University Press and The Newberry Library, 1970), 147.

16. Baird, *Ishmael*, 308.

17. Ibid., 309.

18. Ibid., 309–10.

19. Herman Melville, *Clarel: A Poem and Pilgrimage in the Holy Land*, in *The Writings of Herman Melville*, ed. Harrison Hayford, Alma A. MacDougall, Hershel Parker, and G. Thomas

But nothing, he explains, requires interpretation; the tattoos have no meaning for him, having been thoughtlessly got in youth. So in idle times sailors often get them, some seeking a charm " 'gainst watery doom."[20] Agath, a modern pilgrim's guide to Bethlehem, spies the Holy City from a mountain like a masthead. Like a voice from a later Waste Land he cries "Wreck, ho! the wreck—Jerusalem!"[21] For him Palestine is a bleak island where only tortoises survive. He draws into his shell, feigning death.

Somewhat as "Daniel Orme" has been doing, perhaps. In any case, the story—having long been moribund without ever having really lived—needs serious attention, intensive care. Evidently it is now available from a single English source: Harper & Row's Perennial Classic paperback called *Great Short Works of Herman Melville*,[22] where it is presumably included to justify a claim on the cover, "The Complete Short Stories." Editorially it is dismissed as a "brief exercise in the mode of elegiac commemoration,"[23] which is wrong on all counts save "brief." In 1980 it was appended to a French translation of *Billy Budd, marin*,[24] and until recently it was in the Penguin Melville collection but got dropped. Perhaps the trouble is that full satisfaction with the story depends on the ability and willingness to indulge in a Biographical Heresy.

Everybody used to know that the significance of a literary work lies in the work itself; it does not matter who wrote it or when or under what conditions or why or what the intent. It must not be used for extraneous purposes, either, including, it must be, increased understanding of the author. But that is old stuff. The force of "Daniel Orme" rests substantially in the realization that it is Melville's portrait of himself as an old man approaching death willingly, hoping to depart without remorse, penitence, or confession, and completely

---

Tanselle, Historical and Critical Note by Walter Bezanson (Evanston and Chicago: Northwestern University Press and The Newberry Library, 1991), 389.

20. Ibid., 391.

21. Ibid., 388.

22. *Great Short Works of Herman Melville*, ed. Warner Berthof (New York: Harper & Row, 1969), 424–28.

23. Ibid., 424.

24. Herman Melville, *Billy Budd, marin, suivi de "Daniel Orme,"* trans. Pierre Leyis (Paris: Gallimard, 1980), 171–77.

resigned to obscurity after a life of extraordinary vicissitude and long disappointment. The same tale by an unknown hand would have appeal but lack a telling dimension.

Only essential facts are needed to provide it: that a successful writer in a flood of manic inspiration wrote one of the world's great books only to learn that, having demonstrated his genius, he had lost both audience and livelihood. That he suffered a "breakdown," never recovered his health, and existed in painful, agitated depression for a long time, his many books like rusted guns in the salt air. For a quarter-century he inhabited New York almost invisibly, a $4.00-a-day custom inspector until he was sixty-six and, still without readers, a writer to the end known to few but family.

Few saw him in his long anonymity, fewer recorded the fact. Thus attention focuses of necessity on Julian Hawthorne, who called briefly when Melville was sixty-four, and wrote about the visit four times. This was the occasion on which the sick, thoughtful man told Nathaniel Hawthorne's son that he believed there was an unrevealed secret in his father's life which explained the "gloomy" passages in his books. Julian discounted the idea: "It was characteristic in him to imagine so; there were many secrets untold in his own career."[25] Less well remembered is the picture he provided of Melville: his complete solitude, low voice and manner tightly restrained; his disinclination to talk at all, although he had received Julian for the purpose; his extreme nervousness. "He was a melancholy and pale wraith of what he had been. . . . He seemed partly to shrink . . . and partly to reach out for companionship in the dark region into which his mind was sinking." Asked about a specific literary matter and Julian's father, "he made no intelligible response. His words were vague and indeterminate." Endlessly he opened and closed the same window.[26]

Back in 1851, as Melville, having finished *Moby-Dick*, plunged into *Pierre*, a close friend in Pittsfield reported that he was writing "under a state of morbid excitement which will soon injure his health."[27] His

25. Julian Hawthorne, *Hawthorne and His Circle* (New York: Harper & Brothers, 1930), 33.
26. See Leyda, *The Melville Log*, 2:782–83.
27. This is Sarah Morewood, quoted in Eleanor Melville Metcalf, *Herman Melville: Cycle and Epicycle* (Cambridge: Harvard University Press, 1953), 133.

granddaughter, Mrs. Metcalf, pronounced him already "a sick man" in that year.[28] On publication of the new novel, the *Southern Quarterly Review* called him "clean daft." ("The sooner this author is put in ward the better.")[29] In writing to relatives, his wife, Elizabeth, began stressing his "frightfully nervous state."[30] By 1876 she had to tell even his sisters that for the time being at least they could not visit. Family legend is that, drunk, he pushed her down a flight of stairs.[31] The granddaughter writes of "desperate irascibility and the solace of brandy," the other comfort in the heavily smoked pipes.[32] "He railed against the country at large," she remarks, "to anyone who would listen."[33] She also points out that during the last eight or ten years of his life, retired from his tedious, shadowy job, he grew calmer and quieter, as Arvin would convey in calling attention to "Daniel Orme."

Written contemporary evidence of how sick Melville became did not turn up until the suffering was long over. In 1975 the minister at All Souls Unitarian Church in New York and his assistant printed two memorable letters.[34] In the first, dated May 6, 1867, Elizabeth's half-brother Samuel Shaw of Boston wrote her minister at the church, Henry Bellows, and she responded two weeks later. As the Shaws had long feared and the Melvilles were realizing, the situation for Elizabeth was entirely desperate. Bellows proposed that a kidnapping be staged and she carried off to her Boston relatives. Shaw, a lawyer, urged a legal separation, which her doctor advised. She would simply pay a visit to Boston and stay. The grounds would be her belief in her husband's insanity and that he treated her so ill that she "could not live with him." Her character and religious faith were too strong. She did not take the advice and never had to.

The Melville persona does not have a wife, nor would an average reader suspect that Orme's last home had any counterpart in Melville's late experience. But six months after the plot for Elizabeth's

---

28. Ibid., 135.
29. Leyda, *The Melville Log*, 1:463.
30. Metcalf, *Herman Melville*, 237.
31. Edwin H. Miller, *Melville* (New York: Braziller, 1975), 321.
32. Metcalf, *Herman Melville*, 237.
33. Ibid., 216.
34. Dr. Walter D. Kring and Jonathon S. Carey published their "Two Discoveries Concerning Herman Melville" in *Proceedings of the Massachusetts Historical Society* 87 (1975): 137–41.

escape, Herman's younger brother Thomas, a ship's captain, was elected governor of Sailor's Snug Harbor on the northwest tip of Staten Island. Neither snug nor harbor, it was the grandest institution of its sort in the world, a short voyage by ferry from the southwest tip of Manhattan Island. The view is of upper New York Harbor. A giant row of white Greek Revival buildings (all five completed by Melville's time and now Designated City Landmarks) did not entirely suit Orme's story and nowhere appear in it. But— more evidence of improved spirits—the writer used to visit the place and even spent the night. He regularly attended the annual trustees' banquet and sometimes, by way of reunion, he and his family would dine with Thomas and his. Thomas was the favorite of his mother's living sons, and she preferred Staten Island to the house in town. She and the unmarried sisters moved there, and there mother and Augusta predeceased Herman. A "great haven" he called it in the tale, and not a bad spot to choose for dying.

But loose ends should be tied. For one, "Daniel, or me" is a rude offense against a writer who was clever with puns. "Call me Daniel" would do better, a striking bit of casting for the author in old age. Further, the name had meaning for him, especially the surname. It is uncommon but not unique: Henry James published a story called "Sir Edmund Orme" in the year of Melville's death. Melville had used it before, without the e, in "Pebbles," the last poem in his book *John Marr and Other Sailors* (1888). Orm's appearance is very brief, but he is clearly the same man:

> Old are the creeds, but stale the schools,
>   Revamped as the mode may veer,
> But Orm from the schools to the beaches strays:
> And, finding a Conch hoar with time, he delays
>   And reverent lifts it to ear.

As truth never varies, the sound of ocean "pitched in far monotone" never veers. So, fixed and timeless, are the origins of the old sailor's last name. The clue is the "conch," the Greek root of which is *konko*, shellfish. Orm is a serpent in Icelandic saga, but, as "Pebbles" makes clear, Melville is mindful of mollusks not snakes.

His Orm is short for "Orme," which is short for "ormer," an English word defined in a desk dictionary as an abalone shell. It comes to English via French *ormier*, short for *oreille-de-mer*, ear of the sea, in Latin *auris maris*. An ormer, once meaning the edible part, was thought to be protected from the back by the rock it lived on and in front by its shell, in Daniel's case his unapproachability and the darned Guernsey frock that hides his signs. (Both this seaman's shirt or jacket and the ormer are, oddly, special products of Guernsey. In fact abalones are homeless wanderers by night; when disturbed they grip a rock face with a suction-padded foot of great power.)

Both the Book of Daniel and more Melville are required to account for the rest of Orme's name. The lead appears in *Mardi*, forty years before the story. Taji, narrating, tells of the discovery at sea of a container of superior bisquit:

An oblong box, much battered and bruised, and . . . all over inscriptions and carvings:—foul anchors, skewered hearts, almanacs . . . and divers mystic diagrams in chalk, drawn by old Finnish mariners in casting horoscopes and prophecies. Your old tars are all Daniels.

Not so much prophets this time as interpreters, like the Daniel of chapter V in his book, what was written on the wall (MENE, MENE, TEKEL, UPHARSIN, bad news to the king). And not, of course, that Melville's mariner interprets signs; an old tar, he bears them. Interpretation is left to the viewer. Some suppose scar and tattoo coexist equally, a Melvillean ambiguity. What is meant by saying they "compress the most moving part" of his religious history is not completely clear.

Not opaque, either. On his mother's side, Melville was born into a strict Calvinist tradition, but in liberal Boston his grandfather Melville had grown away from that and his own training. Herman's father and model, Allan, was so convinced of divine guidance that, dying in the midst of financial scandal he had brought on himself by deceit, he counted until almost the end on providential rescue. But the notion that deity controls all for the best led Melville in *Mardi* to serious religious questioning. A year later, in *White-Jacket*, the tendency is

Christian, but the next year in *Moby-Dick* Christ plays no part. The target is God. A French critic in 1853 understood that Ahab chased down the whale because he could not harpoon Him.[35] For mankind, which Melville cared about, Ahab's God has no love whatever; He is an affliction. Religion in *The Confidence-Man* is an ideal front for swindling. In *Clarel* a trip to the Holy Land is crowned at the Church of the Holy Sepulchre—all glitter, no gold, a noxious cheat. Writing of Melville in his notebook back in 1856, Hawthorne had said most of it: "he can neither believe, nor be comfortable in his disbelief; and he is too honest and courageous not to try to do one or the other."[36]

The crisis had come with *Pierre* (1852), when the protagonist discovers at nineteen, as Melville evidently had done,[37] that he has an illegitimate sister. This knowledge was the slash in Melville's spiritual history. "Truth rolls a black billow" through Pierre's Melvillean heart. Knowing the true father (once "beautiful on earth . . . sainted in heaven") means "ruin of the soul's temple." Loss of faith in his father, a God, was loss of faith in God the father. "He holdeth all in the hollow of his hand? A Hollow, truly!"[38] From this point to *Billy Budd* ran the search to replace the parent who abandoned Herman at twelve by dying, and blasted his own memory by having sired a child he never acknowledged. Because it cannot be erased, Orme's tattoo must be canceled—struck—by the scar, not balanced. There is no ambiguity, but at last the achievement of rest in unbelief with eyes, mind, and heart still open.

"Daniel Orme" appears to be the only place in his work where Melville—*in propria persona*, as it were—refers to the possibility of unconfessed guilt and "a dark secret in the past." He throws no light on these matters, but there are known reasons for remorse that Melville as Orme might have suffered in the end, if not "befriended" by that "animal decay" which he says may drowse the conscience. Known as a "strict parent," and apparently an insensitive one, what

35. Braswell, *Melville's Religious Thought*, 59, 137n.
36. Nathaniel Hawthorne, *The English Notebooks*, ed. Randall Stewart (New York: Russell & Russell, 1962), 433.
37. See Chapter 1.
38. Herman Melville, *Pierre; or, The Ambiguities*, ed. Harrison Hayford et al. (Evanston and Chicago: Northwestern University Press and The Newberry Library, 1971), 69, 139.

responsibility he took for his sons, if any, is unknown. Four months after the failed planning for Elizabeth's escape, their Malcolm, eighteen, in his bed at home, shot himself in the head. Stanwix, two years younger, was an Omoo—wanderer, drifter, beachcomber—a misfit. He traveled ceaselessly, jumped ships, tried to be a dentist, herded sheep, and in 1886 died alone at thirty-five in a San Francisco hospital.

Mistreatment of his wife is established. Further, Elizabeth read her husband's books. Written at the very start of their marriage, *Mardi* is the work of a man who does not like women. No one knows what she thought, next year, when she came to *White-Jacket, or The World in a Man-of-War* and pictured a handsome young man, for months at sea on one of those "wooden-walled Gomorrahs of the deep," and "evils so direful that they will hardly bear so much as an allusion."[39] Far down the scale, the failed friendship with Hawthorne may still have weighed. When Orme is drugged and his chest examined, the thought of Chillingworth uncovering the *A* on Dimmesdale's is inevitable. (As a private joke, Hawthorne could have been the Calvinist chaplain who inferred a dark secret in the sailor's past; Orme's last thought is of it.)

As for that "railing against the country at large" to any at hand, it is much to the point that about 1880, reading Arnold's *Empedocles on Etna* (1852), in which the depressed philosopher, lonely and ignored, will kill himself, Melville marked these lines:

> 'T is not the time, 't is not the sophists vex him;
> There is some root of suffering in himself,
> Some secret and unfollowed vein of woe. . . .[40]

Maybe there *was* an unconfessed dark streak of guilt in Melville. But the way of Orme's death positively lifts the spirit anyway, like that of Oedipus at Colonus. And so it is truly curious that his departure is

39. Herman Melville, *White-Jacket, or The World in a Man-of-War*, ed. Harrison Hayford et al. (Evanston and Chicago: Northwestern University Press and The Newberry Library, 1970), 375–76.

40. Quoted by Leon Howard in *Herman Melville* (Berkeley and Los Angeles: University of California Press, 1951), 291.

greatly like and unlike an exit at the end or blackout of *The Confidence-Man*, darkest of Melville's books.

The last chapter of this extraordinary novel introduces the comely, snowy-headed individual who will conclude it. Like Orme, the nameless old fellow is three-score and ten. He is "happily dismissed" from fields to fireplace as Orme from seas to shore. Both men are grateful for solitude. And the nameless one's face, as different from Orme's as his foolish character, is even more remarkable: "A countenance like that which imagination ascribes to good Simeon, when, having at last beheld the Master of Faith, he blessed him and departed in peace."[41] This powerfully invokes the *Nunc dimittis*, a hymn taken from Luke (2:27–32), said or sung at Evening Prayer: "Lord, now lettest thou thy servant depart in peace, according to thy word: / For mine eyes have seen thy salvation." The simple old man is on a riverboat and wants a life preserver for the night. He is given a chamberpot. "But, bless me," he says, "we are being left in the dark. Pah! What a smell, too." Fading light expires. And "in the darkness which ensued, the cosmopolitan kindly led the old man away."[42]

Neither he nor the beached sailor, plainly, has seen salvation. But the end of "Daniel Orme" is a sort of prayer anyhow. Melville is saying his own *Nunc dimittis*. It fades in the hazy air with the dim sails coming or going or at anchor, a part of the natural serenity in which the story dissolves.

41. Herman Melville, *The Confidence-Man*, ed. Harrison Hayford et al. (Evanston and Chicago: Northwestern University Press and The Newberry Library, 1984), 241.
42. Ibid., 251.

Index